DEFENSE STRATEGY IN BRIDGE

Featuring Suit-Preference Signals

by

HY LAVINTHAL

Arranged, Edited and with Quizzes Added by

GEORGE S. COFFIN

DOVER PUBLICATIONS, INC.
NEW YORK

This Book Is Dedicated

To My Wife and Daughter

SYLVIA and EILEEN

Published in Canada by General Publishing Company, Ltd., 30 Lesmill Road, Don Mills, Toronto, Ontario.

This Dover edition, first published in 1974, is an unabridged and corrected republication of the work originally published in 1963 under the title *Defense Tricks*. It is reprinted by special arrangement with George Coffin, Publisher, Waltham, Massachusetts 02154, publisher of the original edition.

International Standard Book Number: 0-486-23010-4
Library of Congress Catalog Card Number: 73-88334

Manufactured in the United States of America
Dover Publications, Inc.
180 Varick Street
New York, N. Y. 10014

INDEX

PUBLISHER'S FOREWORD

Contract Bridge owes its proud lineage to the game of whist. The whist dealer faced the last card to determine trump and his left hand opponent led at once. With no bidding and no dummy to reveal trump length, a player with considerable trump length made a come-on signal or echo in a plain suit, asking partner for a trump lead. Since the advent of Bridge, this signal has been used to direct the lead of the signalling suit itself.

In 1931 Hy Lavinthal noted that the code of defense was of no avail when a switch to a specific suit was urgent. This led him to find a way which did not conflict with normal signals. Thus was born the new wonder weapon of defense, the suit-preference signal.

One year later Hy Lavinthal submitted his signal to the late Ely Culbertson to confirm its worth. Culbertson approved it in his *Red Book on Play*, — and in the *Bridge World* of June 1934 Hy Lavinthal's article introduced this new signal. This signal is properly called the Lavinthal.

This new book shows how Hy Lavinthal has broadened the effectiveness of his signal, *covering situations where heretofore it was impossible to relay information.* Both average and top-flight players have much to gain from this book, — so much so that they cannot afford to dispense with the Lavinthal.

PREFACE

This book assumes that the reader has an elementary knowledge of how the game of bridge is played and that he is concerned with learning how to convey more vital information which will guide his partner to the winning line of defense.

Forty years have passed since the development of suit-preference signals. In the time intervening use has proven their effectiveness in many situations where primary signals are of no avail. Today the great majority of experts use the suit-preference signal because they have found it indispensable. They refrain from the use of this signal only when playing with partners who lack the knowledge of how to use this defensive weapon.

The examples and discussions have two main purposes. First, they show how the use of suit-preference signals broadens the scope of effective information relayed to the partner, — without impairing the use of primary signals. Second, you learn how in many situations the suit-preference signal is the only means of discovering the winning line of play. WHAT MIGHT HAVE BEEN A GUESS, IS NOW TRANSFORMED INTO A CERTAINTY.

Simple logic identifies the situation where the suit-preference signal can be employed and the message clearly understood by the partner. When so used, the signal card can never be read as a primary signal.

Check the examples to see if my statements bear me out. I am sure that you will then appreciate the advantage which a defending partnership can gain by the proper use of suit-preference signals.

The use of suit-preference signals constitutes a second line of defense and does not abrogate the use of primary signals. In fact, in many situations the complementary use of both types of signals will relay information to a partner which can produce the equivalent to double-dummy defense.

Over-enthusiasm for suit-preference signals can lead to their abuse and consequent loss to a partnership. For a sure profit employ a suit-preference signal only when a clear opportunity presents itself. Yet always be alert lest opportunity catches you napping.

The suit-preference signal is a fine tool for good players. Its adoption by an alert partnership will take the guess out of many situations. As time goes on, the application of suit-preference signals will be accepted as a necessary prelude to masterful defensive play because a good partnership cannot afford to dispense with its advantages.

HY LAVINTHAL

Trenton, New Jersey

THE CODE OF DEFENSE

The primary code of defense is the lifeblood of defensive play. Without it defenders would work at cross purposes and only in rare cases could they make the best use of their combined resources. This code of signals enables the defenders to play effectively, — especially when they couple its use with good judgment.

Declarer and his opponents try to turn to their respective advantage inferences derived from the auction. Later in the play each defender is constantly striving to visualize the cards remaining in his partner's hand.

Each defender, through implications revealed by the code of the defense, can get a good picture of the cards held by his partner. This code of defense is so named because each card faced by the defenders reveals more than just its denomination. The story told by defenders' cards lets the defenders join forces and make good use of the cards at their disposal.

A keen defender paired with an equally adept partner can soon visualize how to make the best use of their cards. The data, which they relay to each other on the first few tricks, is simply the prelude to a course of action which shows the best promise of winning the most tricks.

The two partners on defense must keep this thought constantly in mind. IT IS OF UTMOST IMPORTANCE TO FIND THE WINNING LINE OF DEFENSE, IF IT EXISTS, AS SOON AS POSSIBLE. This thought should govern the choice of the opening lead as well as the subsequent play. Should the opening lead be unfortunate, the defenders must try to uncover an alternate defense which shows promise.

Both defenders know that declarer is listening in on messages which they relay to each other. So a good defender on occasion will withhold certain information from his partner. This exercise of good judgment is the prerogative of either defender, whenever it appears to be in the best defensive interest. Just as the defenders can err for lack of data, so can declarer err when he chooses a losing line of play from not knowing how unseen key cards are dispersed.

On many hands the code of defense effectively pictures the defenders' concealed holdings and at the same time how each defender wants his partner to proceed. Wherever the code of defense fails to reveal a promising course of action, each defender when on lead must rely on what he thinks is the best line of play. In every bridge session hands occur during whose first few tricks one defender is baffled when the best policy seems to call for a lead in another suit. The defender on lead knows that the fate of this hand may rest upon his decision. It is not enough for him to know that he must shift to another suit. The lack of timely guidance may cause him to shift to the wrong suit and the chance to retrieve his misjudgment may never come again. If you have played bridge any length of time, you can easily recall when either you or your partner, having no guidance, made the wrong switch.

Suppose that defenders use primary signals only. Declarer gets to 4 ♡ with no other suit mentioned. Fortunately, your partner overcalled 1 ♠ which simplifies your opening lead of the ♠ A. Dummy shows a singleton spade and many trumps. Retaining the lead, you note that partner played his lowest spade. The first inference is that your partner wants you to quit spades, out of which grows the negative inference, — SHIFT TO ANOTHER SUIT. All this is obvious without a message from partner. What you lack and would like to have is a message that would reveal which side suit your partner wants led. Because primary signals have their limitations, this fateful decision is yours alone. So you are forced to make what appears to be the best guess.

In this and in many other situations, the lack of competent direction reveals the necessity of a signalling device which will complement the primary code of defence and offer help.

PRIMARY SIGNALS WERE DESIGNED TO CONVEY INFERENCES WHICH COULD DESCRIBE ONLY THE SUIT LED OR PLAYED.

In the first few tricks, when the fate of the hand is in balance, the primary lead or follow-suit signal cannot designate the lead of another specific suit. If such a situation arose once in a blue moon, I would be the first to concede that there was no need for a suit-preference signal.

In order better to cope with declarer and not to be at a disadvantage, the defenders have a new weapon, — the suit-preference signal. With its aid it is no longer necessary to rely upon wishful thinking or upon a sheer guess.

The need for a signalling device which would make up for this lack of guidance came to me forcefully in the deal on page 12.

Back in 1931 when in slam bidding there was no wholesale ace-showing convention, I was foolhardy enough to barge into 6 ♡. Even in this day and age, modern players who know better disdain Blackwood and land in slams off two aces. (Please turn to page 12.)

SUMMARY OF SUIT-PREFERENCE SIGNALS

Whereas the message transmitted by a primary signal refers to the signalling suit itself, a suit-preference signal is made to direct the lead of ANOTHER SPECIFIC SUIT. This signal is made early, usually before the fifth trick.

A suit-preference signal pinpoints one of two suits other than trumps (or declarer's running suit at no-trump) and the suit in which the signal is made.

The lead or play of an unnecessarily high card directs the lead of the higher ranking of the other two suits. Conversely, the lead or play of the lowest card directs the lead of the lower ranking of the other two suits. A Middle card (not a SPS) suggests disinterest in choice.

Key to the Species

1. *Lavinthal Follow-Suit SPS.* A defender plays an unnecessarily high card or his lowest card to signal a preference for another specific suit.

2. *Lavinthal Lead SPS.* A defender leads an unnecessarily high card or his lowest card to signal a preference for another specific suit.

3. *Lavinthal Discard SPS.* A defender's first high or lowest discard specifies which one of the other two suits should be led by partner.

4. *Lavinthal Unusual SPS.* A defender makes a lead or play, recognizable as contrary to accepted use, to emphasize suit-preference.

I. FOLLOW-SUIT SIGNALS

Deal 1 Basic Lavinthal

North
♠ K 6
♡ Q 10 8 6 5
◇ 10 9 4
♣ Q J 10

West	East
♠ A 10 9 7 3 2	♠ J 8 5 4
♡ ——	♡ 2
◇ 8 6 5 2	◇ K 7
♣ 9 8 7	♣ A 6 5 4 3 2

South
♠ Q
♡ A K J 9 7 4 3
◇ A Q J 3
♣ K

South	West	North	East
1 ♡	1 ♠	2 ♡	2 ♠
6 ♡!	Pass	Pass	Pass

Opening the ♠ A, West saw the four and Queen drop. Clearly the four was his partner's lowest spade, a discouraging signal. It offered the inference of a switch to another suit. Which minor suit should West now lead? Fearful of dummy's scare cards in clubs, West led a diamond to the King and I won with the Ace. I drew trumps and parked my club loser on the ♠ K, making my rash slam.

This hand pinpointed the inadequacy of primary defense signals in situations requiring a switch to ONE PARTICULAR SUIT. With no way of asking partner for a club lead, East could only hope that West would make a good guess.

Being of an inquiring mind, I tried to devise a way to enable a defender to guide his partner to switch to a specific suit whenever urgent.

After mulling it over, I discovered the way. In this particular hand, on West's spade lead a high or low spade signal by East to picture his spade holding would be valueless against dummy's spade control. What was needed was some means to direct a switch to a specific suit. I saw the daylight when this solution came to me.

If the primary inference of a card is useless, why not endow high and low cards with a secondary function to direct the lead of a specific suit?

By excluding trumps and the suit led, you have a simple way to show preference by rank for one of the remaining two suits. If East wants a club led, he follows with his lowest spade; if he wants a diamond, he plays an unnecessarily high spade, THE HIGHEST THAT HE CAN AFFORD. An obvious middle card could be read as indicating no preference. Thus was born a new defensive weapon.

In the hand above East would follow suit with his LOWEST spade to ask for a club lead.

Contract bridge has become a more fascinating game because the SPS has given the defenders a sense of balance and more equality in their battle against declarer.

Suit-preference signals are confined mostly to the early play of the hand. Late in the play defenders must rely solely upon primary signals. Often in the middle or end-game, one or both defenders are hard pressed for discards. If the proper defense cannot be found, nothing will avail.

In those rare ambiguous situations, the primary inference of a signal outranks suit preference. A review of the auction and in nearly every case common sense will furnish the clue to the proper interpretation.

The main function of all signals is to clarify and help determine the right line of defensive play. The pre-requisite to the effective use of SPS is that both defenders understand how and when to use primary signals. Only then will they have no difficulty in recognizing special situations where SPS can gain.

Also both defenders must co-operate. In defense the human equation is important. If one unfortunately draws a partner who pays no attention to cards as played, and/or if this partner does not bother to read the inferences offered by your carding, you must confine your signals to simple situations and hope that he sees them. This is important.

It must be clear that the suit-preference signals constitute a second line of defense. They do not infringe upon the realm of primary signals, for their sole purpose it to complement them when clearly the lead or play of a high or low card cannot be misunderstood.

The preceding deal led me to explore the effectiveness of the SPS in other defensive positions. It must not infringe upon the useful functions of primary signals. The SPS is used only in situations WHERE PRIMARY SIGNALS ARE CLEARLY INEFFECTIVE. The ever-increasing acceptance of the SPS by strong players has proved its value.

Throughout this book you will find hands, each demonstrating a different situation where a SPS offers the only clue to the winning line of defense. The SPS can be made on follow-suit cards, leads and discards, — in both trump and notrump contracts.

This defensive weapon permits defenders to cope with declarer on more equal terms. Before the advent of the SPS, declarer could make many contracts which today would not stand a ghost of a chance against defenders using the SPS.

If suit-preference signals are meaningless to your partner, do not expect him to read them.

When one opens the bidding, the normal expectation is quick entries in the bid suit. Contract bridge owes its fascination to the fact that the unexpected can happen, as on the next deal. Suit preference was the key to the winning defense.

Deal 2 Unexpected Fun

North:
♠ 10 7 5
♡ 3 2
♢ 7 4 3
♣ A K Q J 4

West:
♠ A 6 3
♡ 9 8 6 5
♢ Q 10 8 5 2
♣ 2

East:
♠ 9 2
♡ K J 10 7 4
♢ A K
♣ 10 8 6 3

South:
♠ K Q J 8 4
♡ A Q
♢ J 9 6
♣ 9 7 5

West	North	East	South
Pass	Pass	1 ♡	1 ♠
2 ♡	2 ♠	Pass	3 ♠
4 ♡	4 ♠ (final bid)		

From the auction East expected a heart lead. Contrary to expectation West opened the ♣ 2 which could be read as a singleton. With the defenders using SPS, it was up to East to show his partner how to build a ruffing position into extra tricks. The ♣ 2 declarer won in dummy and East followed with the THREE. This pleased West, a SPS telling where his partner held a quick entry. The ♣ 3 asked partner to lead the lower ranking of the other two plain suits, — in this case a diamond.

Declarer led a low spade to the king and West won with the ace. Faced with no guess, thanks to East's lowest club play, West led a diamond to East's King. East returned a club which West ruffed. West returned another diamond to East's ace and got another club ruff, and finally cashed the ◇ Q. Declarer won the balance but he was set three tricks.

Without a SPS, one might accuse West of peeking. How else would he know to return a diamond rather than a heart?

If not playing suit preference, West at trick three would lead a heart because East had bid hearts. Declarer would draw trumps and take 11 tricks.

The ability to read the shape of declarer's hand from the bidding is often vital in the search for the setting trick. On the next deal an alert defender took advantage of opponents' precise bidding.

Deal 3, E-W vul. Too Much Science

West	North	East
	♠ Q J 7 ♡ Q J 5 ◇ A Q 8 7 5 4 ♣ 2	
♠ 9 3 ♡ 6 2 ◇ 10 9 6 2 ♣ A J 8 5 3		♠ A 6 5 ♡ A 8 7 ◇ J 3 ♣ K 9 7 6 4
	♠ K 10 8 4 2 ♡ K 10 9 4 3 ◇ K ♣ Q 10	

West	North	East	South
——	1 ◇	Pass	1 ♠
Pass	2 ◇	Pass	2 ♡
Pass	2 ♠	Pass	4 ♠
Pass	Pass	Pass	

Scientific bidding can boomerang. If North simply raises 1 ♠ to 2 ♠ instead of rebidding diamonds,

South will jump to 4 ♠ and so conceal his 5-5 shape from prying defenders. While the question is close, telling everything makes things easier for the defenders.

West opens the ♣ A. The lone club in dummy was like a "Stop, Look and Listen" sign at a railroad crossing. From the auction East figured that probably declarer held five hearts. Hence West held a doubleton and a chance to ruff.

So on the ♣ A East played his NINE, an unnecessarily high club as suit preference for a heart lead. Reading this, West switched to the ♡ 6. East won with the Ace and fired back a heart to void West of hearts.

Declarer took the second heart and lost a trump honor to East's Ace. East shot back his third heart to let West ruff and defeat declarer.

Or East could duck the first heart, — later play ♡ A then low to let West ruff. In some deals such a duck is vital for entry reasons. If West holds the ♠ A instead of East, the heart duck is crucial. After declarer drives out West's trump Ace, East would need transport via a low heart from West to the ace to get in and give West a heart ruff.

In the initial play of the hand, suit preference is indicated if either defender makes an irregular lead or play which is recognizable. In the next deal note how scientific bidding led to declarer's downfall.

Deal 4 Stayman Clue

North:
♠ J 3 2
♡ K Q 10 7 4
◇ Q 8
♣ Q 8 3

West:
♠ 8 5
♡ A 5
◇ 9 7 6 4 3
♣ 10 9 7 2

East:
♠ K Q 10 9 4
♡ 8 6 3 2
◇ A 2
♣ 5 4

South:
♠ A 7 6
♡ J 9
◇ K J 10 5
♣ A K J 6

South	West	North	East
1 NT	Pass	2 ♣*	Pass
2 ◇	Pass	3 ♡	Pass
3 NT	Pass	Pass	Pass

West led the ♠ 8, dummy ducked and East overtook with his nine. Declarer held up the ♠ A so East returned the ♠ K which declarer won with the Ace. Declarer led the ♡ J which West ducked. West needed some tangible clue from his partner. West got it for

* Kempson Convention, in the USA usually called "Stayman Over Notrump."

East dropped the EIGHTSPOT. The Stayman clue was South's 2 ♢ response to 2 ♣, DENYING four heart cards. Clearly East must hold three or four hearts and the ♡ 8 was not a forced play but was a voluntary card.

The only purpose of this high card, the ♡ 8, was suit preference. East intended to direct his partner to lead the higher ranking of the other two suits, in this case a diamond. East also knew that West had no spade left and the need for a diamond lead was urgent.

West's ♡ A won the next lead and East played the ♡ 2, confirming suit preference. With all the high cards in dummy, West knew that his partner was not playing his hearts as a simple echo in declarer's suit to show a doubleton. This was not an effort to shut out dummy's long hearts.

So West led a diamond which East won with the Ace, and East cashed three more spade tricks to break the contract.

For instructional purposes let us switch the minor suits in all four hands. Give East ♢ 5-4 and ♣ A-2. To indicate suit preference for the lower ranking of the other two suits excluding spades, East on the first heart lead would play his LOWEST heart, the deuce; then the EIGHTSPOT. Looking for the ♡ 3 and ♡ 6, West would know that both these cards could not be missing from East's hand, hence read East's suit preference for a club lead.

The purpose of a suit-preference signal is to direct the lead of a specific suit. This does not imply that the defender has a good trick in the suit that he wants led. In the next deal the SPS directed a lead in a suit where nothing could be lost. Later declarer guessed wrong with a two-way finesse against a queen.

Deal 5, N-S vul. Avoiding A Trap

West	North	East
	♠ J 2 ♡ Q J 7 4 3 ◇ A J 4 ♣ K J 6	
♠ K Q 8 7 4 ♡ 8 ◇ 9 6 5 ♣ 9 8 7 3		♠ 10 9 6 3 ♡ 10 ◇ Q 10 8 7 ♣ Q 5 4 2
	♠ A 5 ♡ A K 9 6 5 2 ◇ K 3 2 ♣ A 10	

South	West	North	East
1 ♡	1 ♠ (?)	3 ♡	3 ♠
6 ♡	Pass	Pass	Pass

West's bad 1 ♠ overcall is the sort of tactic that leads to one thing, — writing home for more money.

But West had the luck of the Irish and it helped in this case.

West opened the ♠ K which declarer won with the ace. Declarer drew trumps, then exited in spades to eliminate spades from both his hands. West won the trick with ♠ Q and East realized that his partner would be in a quandary for his next lead. So East came up with the ♠ 10. Knowing that the ♠ 10 was not a forced card, West read the intent of suit preference and returned a low diamond because his partner wanted a lead in the higher ranking of the two other plain suits. Dummy inserted the jack, East covered with the queen and declarer won with the king. Later declarer finessed the ♣ 10 the wrong way and East's queen scored the setting trick.

Without the SPS, West to trick four could as readily shift to a club, relieving declarer's problem. With clubs giving him three tricks, he would be able to park a diamond on the third club trick. The slam contract would be in the bag, thanks to a wrong defensive guess.

The popular short 1 ♣ and 1 ♢ bid often masks the location of high cards. On the next deal North opened 1 ♣ and later his partner supported clubs. If you were West in this auction, would you think that your partner held ♣ A-Q? No. A suit-preference signal on West's opening lead corrected this impression. *Again, suit-preference came to the rescue.*

Deal 6 — A Right View

North:
♠ K 10 7 5
♡ Q 8 6
♢ A Q 7
♣ K 9 5

West:
♠ 8 6
♡ A 9 7
♢ 8 6 5 4 3 2
♣ 6 3

East:
♠ Q 3
♡ K J 10 5 2
♢ 10 9
♣ A Q 7 2

South:
♠ A J 9 4 2
♡ 4 3
♢ K J
♣ J 10 8 4

South	West	North	East
——	——	1 ♣	1 ♡
1 ♠	Pass	2 ♠	Pass
3 ♣	Pass	3 ♠	(final bid)

West opened the ♡ A. When dummy was spread, East upgraded his club holding. The extra prospect that West could ruff the third club lead prompted East to follow with the TWO of hearts. West read it as suit preference for a lead in clubs, the lower ranking of the other two plain suits. West did not confuse the ♡ 2 play as a usual discouraging card. West knew that his partner held plenty of hearts, which made it simple to designate a switch to a specific suit.

So West led a club and East took two club tricks at once. East noted that West led the ♣ 6 then played ♣ 3. With the ♣ 2 staring him in the face, East led a third club, knowing that his partner would ruff. This West did. Adding insult to injury, West shifted back to hearts and his partner took the setting trick there.

Without a SPS at trick one, West would never have shifted to a club. A diamond switch would be disastrous. Cashing ten tricks, declarer would berate himself for not bidding game.A diamond lead to trick two lets declarer win in hand, lay down ♠ A and ♠ K to draw trumps, then cash two more diamond tricks and get a heart discard. Declarer would return to hand via a trump and finesse the ♣ J. East would cash two club tricks, but mourn for two tricks that flew the coop, a club ruff and the second heart trick.

A SPS often insures an otherwise unlikely yet vital lead. If East had preferred a diamond lead to trick two, he would have played the ♡ J to trick one.

But how would East ask West to continue hearts? In this case East would play a MIDDLE card, the ♡ 5.

To differentiate a SPS from a primary come-on signal in an obvious five-card or longer suit, make the SPS with either the LOWEST CARD or the HIGHEST CARD at your disposal, *so long as you know that it will not cause the loss of a trick in that suit.*

In Deal 7 at rubber bridge North and South had a part score of 40 points. North and South were interested only in a cheap safe contract to score their game by addition.

Deal 7, N-S vul. plus 40 Second Best

West	North	East
	♠ K 4 3 ♡ K 7 5 ◇ K 9 8 7 ♣ K 6 3	
♠ J 10 8 5 2 ♡ A 6 ◇ Q J 4 ♣ Q 10 2		♠ A Q ♡ 9 8 4 2 ◇ 10 6 5 3 2 ♣ 9 4
	♠ 9 7 6 ♡ Q J 10 3 ◇ A ♣ A J 8 7 5	

South	West	North	East
1 ♣	1 ♠	1 NT	Pass
2 ♣	Pass	3 ♣	(final bid)

West opened the ♠ J, dummy ducked, so East won with the queen. Next East cashed the ♠ A. By simple logic West knew that East now had no spade left. West saw a chance to gain an extra trick by giving his partner a suit-preference signal, so on trick two he followed suit with the TEN OF SPADES. East noted this unnecessarily high spade, and in compliance with his partner's cue, led a heart. West played his ace and returned a spade, and East ruffed the king. Later West scored his natural trump trick that broke the contract.

If not playing the SPS, East might have shifted to a diamond at trick three, letting declarer in to lay down the ace and king of trumps. Declarer would concede one trump trick and the ♡ A, but he would score game.

Whenever an honor card or a combination of honors in one suit are dealt without any low card of the same suit, such honors are said to be dry. A singleton ace is also called a dry ace.

A dry ace-king is rare, yet when held a defender leads the ace first then the king as a standard down-and-out signal. Often the purpose is to show partner the ability to ruff.

Deal 8 Ace-King Dry

West	North	East
	♠ K 9 7 6	
	♡ J 6 3	
	◇ 7 6	
	♣ Q J 4 3	
♠ 10 8 5		♠ 3
♡ 9 8 7 4		♡ A Q 5 2
◇ 10 8 4 3		◇ Q 9 5 2
♣ A K		♣ 10 9 6 5
	♠ A Q J 4 2	
	♡ K 10	
	◇ A K J	
	♣ 8 7 2	

The auction went: South 1 ♠, North 2 ♠; and South jumped to 4 ♠, finis.

West opened the ♣ A, right from ace-king dry. East, having no interest in clubs, played the ♣ 5. To the second trick West led the ♣ K and East perked up fast. East now knew that West was dry in clubs. To let his partner know that on the next trick a heart should be led, East gave a suit-preference signal by following with the ten, his best club. West noted his partner's play of an unnecessarily high club and he was thankful for the SPS. Certain that his partner wanted the higher ranking of the other two plain suits led, West led a heart. East won with the ♡ A and returned a club which West ruffed for the setting trick.

Declarer had no use for suit preference. He knew that before the advent of SPS, he would have had an even chance of fulfilling his contract. At trick three a diamond shift lets declarer get home.

♠ ♡ ◇ ♣ ◇ ♡ ♠ ♡ ◇ ♣ ◇ ♡ ♠

WORLD'S GREATEST TOURNAMENT DIRECTOR

George W. Benyon (1864–1965) was the Grand Old Man of duplicate bridge. He played pro lacrosse and hockey, then conducted symphony orchestras until the crash in 1929, when he switched to bridge. He was an ACBL tournament director and editor of the *ACBL Bulletin* until he retired in 1955 at the age of 90. Asked at his retirement dinner why he lived so long, he replied, "I never drink . . . (long pause) . . . water." He added, "I will see you at my one hundredth anniversary." And he did! For more details, see *Encyclopedia of Bridge*, third revised edition of 1971, p. 567.

For three decades his *Bridge Director's Manual* has been the bible of the ACBL tournament directors. It has been revised completely seven times (seventh edition 1965). An eighth, posthumous, edition is being planned.

♠ ♡ ◇ ♣ ◇ ♡ ♠ ♡ ◇ ♣ ◇ ♡ ♠

Wishful thinking is better than no thinking at all. Holding a worthless hand is no excuse for a defender to relax and wait for the next hand. On the next deal a defender with a Yarborough found the only way to defeat declarer.

Deal 9 Futile Tenace

West	North	East
	♠ K	
	♡ 8 6 5 4	
	◇ Q 10 8 7 2	
	♣ J 10 4	
♠ A J 10 4 3		♠ 9 8 7 6 2
♡ A 7		♡ 9 3
◇ J 3		◇ 9 6 5 4
♣ A Q 8 5		♣ 7 6
	♠ Q 5	
	♡ K Q J 10 2	
	◇ A K	
	♣ K 9 3 2	

South	West	North	East
1 ♡	Double	3 ♡	Pass
Pass	Double	Pass	3 ♠
4 ♡	Double	(final bid)	

Perhaps West's double of 4 ♡ was unwise. Luckily West had an imaginative partner who could bail him out of trouble.

West opened the ♠ A, catching dummy's lone king. Looking at a Yarborough, which was probably too balanced to do any damage, East paused to see if he could help. After all, his partner's predicament was also his own. East felt that his partner must have sound values, probably including a trump trick, — for two takeout doubles topped by a penalty double.

East saw a glimmer of daylight if his partner held something like the ♣ A or ♣ K-Q. His plan formulated, East played his LOWEST spade on the ♠ A opening.

West noted East's call for the lead of the lower ranking of the other two plain suits, a club. Hence West broke his futile club tenace by leading the ♣ A. On this East played the encouraging ♣ 7, and West continued with a low club which dummy's ten won.

Declarer re-entered his hand via the ♢ A. He cashed the ♠ Q which let him pitch off dummy's last club. Next declarer led the ♡ 10, his lowest trump honor, hoping that if West held the ace, that worthy would duck. But West hopped up with the ♡ A and returned a club that dummy trumped high but East over-ruffed with the ♡ 9 for the setting trick.

Rubbing Aladdin's lamp brought its just reward to East. But West commented as he glowed with victory, "Miracles do happen. As I told you before, my penalty doubles are as solid as the Rock of Gibraltar." East smiled and never said a word.

In every duplicate game at least one hand occurs where the bidding is high, wide and handsome. On the next deal no North-South pair let its opponents play for less than 5 ♡. Note that East-West can win 12 tricks at hearts, a difficult slam to bid.

Deal 10, E-W vul. Better Score

North
♠ J 9 8 3 2
♡ 5 4
◇ K J 9
♣ K J 3

West
♠ 7 5
♡ A 9 6 3
◇ 6 5 4 3 2
♣ 6 2

East
♠ 6
♡ K Q J 10 7 2
◇ A Q 10
♣ A 8 4

South
♠ A K Q 10 4
♡ 8
◇ 8 7
♣ Q 10 9 7 5

West	North	East	South
——	——	1 ♡	1 ♠
Pass	2 ♠	3 ♡	3 ♠
4 ♡	4 ♠	5 ♡	5 ♠
Pass	Pass	Double	(final bid)

At the duplicate game where this deal came up, two North-South pairs persisted to 5 ♠ over 5 ♡ and they were doubled. One East-West pair was using suit-preference signals, and got a better result.

In this playoff West opened the ♡ A and his partner followed suit with the ♡ K. The message conveyed was unmistakably suit preference, directing a lead from the higher ranking of the other two plain suits. West led a diamond to trick two. So the defense won two diamond tricks plus the ♡ A and ♣ A for a two-trick set.

Had East desired a club lead, he would have played the ♡ 2 to trick one. Had East wanted another heart lead, his partner would know by East's play of a middle card, in this case the ♡ 7. Thus with a suit-preference signal you can receive a broad range of data whenever you definitely know that partner has good length in his suit. Only a diamond lead to trick two can hold declarer to nine tricks.

Using primary signals only, East would play the ♡ 2 on the ♡ A opening, a discouraging signal suggesting a shift. West, in a quandary, might guess wrong and lead a club, hoping forlornly to ruff the third club lead. Declarer would get in and draw trumps, and finally discard two diamonds from dummy on his own long club suit.

Suit-preference signals oftimes owe their effectiveness to the groundwork that has been prepared by primary signals. The next deal well illustrates how primary and SPS complement each other in the quest for the winning line of defense.

Deal 11 The Sneaky Spade

West	North	East
	♠ Q 9 6	
	♡ 7 4	
	◇ K 9 3	
	♣ Q J 7 5 3	
♠ 4		♠ A K J 10 3
♡ Q J 10 9 3		♡ 6 5 2
◇ 8 7 5 4 2		◇ J 6
♣ A 4		♣ 9 6 2
	♠ 8 7 5 2	
	♡ A K 8	
	◇ A Q 10	
	♣ K 10 8	

South opened 1 NT, North raised to 2 NT; and South rebid 3 NT, end.

West opened the ♡ Q which declarer won with the king. East discouraged a further heart lead by following suit with the ♡ 2. Declarer attacked clubs leading the king first. West ducked to watch what card his partner would play. It was the NINE of clubs, suggesting a signal. When declarer lost the next club to West's ace, West noted the ♣ 6 fall from his partner. completing an echo.

This could be the usual down-and-out signal to show a doubleton in declarer's club suit. The purpose is to hold up the ace (if held) to block entry to the suit in dummy. However, with the ◇ K visible in dummy, which looks like a quick entry, a blocking signal has no purpose and East's ♣ 9 should be interpreted otherwise.

West read the club echo as a suit-preference signal, directing the lead of the higher ranking of the other two suits. West knew that East could make this distinction after playing the ♡ 2 on the opening lead. Of the two remaining suits, the spades ranked higher, to which West switched. With the hearts obviously marooned for lack of entry, the direction afforded by East's SPS was most opportune. The spade lead trapped the queen and East cashed five spade tricks to set declarer two tricks.

"Sneaky lead, that spade," commented declarer.

What would East imply if he played his clubs bottom up? The normal order in such a delicate position could imply a preference, or it could have no meaning. Certainly IT WOULD DENY INTEREST IN SPADES.

At times one must decide whether to read partner's card as a primary signal or as a suit-preference signal. In rare cases ambiguity can occur, but in nearly all situations a review of the bidding and/or cards in view in dummy will clarify the intent.

Deal 12 — Right Clue

North:
♠ A 6 2
♡ K J
◇ K Q J 8 7 3
♣ J 5

West:
♠ Q 10 9 7 3
♡ A 9 5
◇ 10 5
♣ 10 4 3

East:
♠ K 5
♡ 8 7 6 4
◇ A 2
♣ 9 8 7 6 2

South:
♠ J 8 4
♡ Q 10 3 2
◇ 9 6 4
♣ A K Q

West	North	East	South
——	1 ◇	Pass	1 ♡
Pass	2 ◇	Pass	2 NT
Pass	3 NT	(final bid)	

West opened the ♠ 10 and dummy played low. East won with the king and returned the ♠ 5, drawing the eightspot, nine and ace.

Declarer paused to review his chances. If West had held five spades and East held both red aces, nothing could stop declarer from making 3 NT. If West held the ♢ A, nothing could save declarer from defeat. However, if East held the ♢ A and kindly made the probable club return, the contract would be in the bag.

Hoping for Lady Luck to favor him, declarer led the ♢ K which East ducked, and West played the TEN of diamonds. The next diamond lead lost to East's ace, and East saw the ♢ 5 fall from his partner's hand. Now East had to decide whether West's high-low play of ♢ 10-5 was an echo, showing a doubleton, — or if the intent of the ten play was suit preference. East quickly rejected the former because this echo should be made only when dummy seems to have no entry except in diamonds. With hearts bid by declarer, the ♡ K-J should provide entry. Certain that the ♢ 10 play was a SPS, directing the lead of the higher ranking of the other two suits, EAST MADE THE UNATTRACTIVE HEART LEAD. West won this with the ♡ A and cashed three more spade tricks to set declarer two tricks.

Some bridge players decry suit-preference signals for showing a profit only in rare hands. This premise is false, for a chance to gain by a SPS arises three to five times per bridge session. The next deal is from a match-point duplicate.

Deal 13 The Proud Jack

West	North	East
	♠ Q 6 ♡ 4 ◇ K J 9 4 2 ♣ K J 9 8 3	
♠ K 7 ♡ Q 10 7 5 3 ◇ 7 6 3 ♣ 7 6 4		♠ 5 4 2 ♡ K J 9 8 2 ◇ A Q 10 ♣ 5 2
	♠ A J 10 9 8 3 ♡ A 6 ◇ 8 5 ♣ A Q 10	

South	West	North	East
1 ♠	Pass	2 ◇	Pass
3 ♠	Pass	4 ♠	(final bid)

West opened the ♡ 5 to king and ace. Next declarer ruffed his ♡ 6 in dummy, and West dropped the ♡ 3. East, last to play on this trick, almost had a perfect picture of how the cards were distributed. So on this trick East played his proud jack.

Why the JACK of hearts? As the hearts fell, East was checking every inference. With declarer's jump rebid in spades, West's opening ♡ 5 lead looked like a fourth best. With the play to trick two, East felt sure that his partner had not led doubleton ♡ 5-3. If it were, declarer would hold ♡ A-Q-10-7-6 and would have bid hearts. Hence East's proud ♡ J on trick two was informative as well as safe.

In turn how could West read the ♡ J as a SPS for the higher ranking of the other two plain suits, in this case the diamond suit? West reasoned that if East's ♡ J play was forced, declarer started life with ♡ A-9-8-6-2. This is improbable because declarer FAILED to bid hearts. So West knew that East was asking for a diamond lead.

Declarer led the ♠ Q from dummy and lost the finesse to West's king. Not having to guess, West led the ◇ 7 so East cashed his two top diamonds. Declarer made his contract but gained few match points. Had West guessed wrong and led a club, declarer would have won two extra tricks for a top score.

Every once in a while a hand crops up that proves that the play of the hand is more rewarding than the bidding. Sometimes declarer is commended for his superior play; sometimes defenders gain admiration of their opponents for countering what might have been a winning declarer play.

Deal 14 Grand Larceny

♠ J 5 2
♡ Q 6 5
◇ Q J 10 3
♣ K J 6

♠ 9 7 6
♡ 9 4 3
◇ A K 9 7 6
♣ 9 3

♠ A Q 10 3
♡ J 10 7 2
◇ 8 5 4 2
♣ 10

♠ K 8 4
♡ A K 8
◇ —
♣ A Q 8 7 5 4 2

West	North	East	South
—	—	Pass	1 ♣
Pass	1 NT	Pass	3 ♣
Pass	4 ♣	Pass	6 ♣
Pass	Pass	Pass	

The 1 NT response to a 1 ♣ opening bid shows

9 to 11 high-card points, yet denies a biddable major suit. Look at the North and South hands. How can declarer hope to make his ambitious 6 ♣ contract?

In a duplicate game two pairs bid the slam as shown above. At both tables West opened the ◇ K which declarer ruffed. Each declarer appraised his remote chances, but saw a ray of hope. Dummy's diamond honors could produce two tricks by a swindle if one honor is lost early to West and he fails to find the spade return.

Both declarers were strong players and past masters of grand larceny at the bridge table. They realized that an optical illusion could be created that might induce West to return a heart.

So at each table declarer entered dummy via the ♣ K and rightly refrained from drawing another trump lest East discard a high spade to signal his ace. Next each declarer led the ◇ Q and from his own closed hand discarded the EIGHTSPOT of hearts to feign weakness in hearts. West won the ◇ Q with his ace.

At this point one defending partnership failed to find the winning play because East had no way of telling partner to lead a spade. Lacking any indication from his partner, West swallowed declarer's bait and returned a heart to declarer's great joy. Declarer won this trick with the ♡ A and cashed the trump ace on which East tossed the ♠ 10 to show the ♠ A, but it was too late. Next came the ♡ K to unblock. Declarer entered dummy via the ♣ J and won the ♡ Q and ◇ J-10 for three spade discards. Grand larceny paid off.

At both tables the sequence of plays to the first three tricks was the same until declarer led the ◇ Q from dummy. At the second table East played his EIGHTSPOT, an unnecessarily high card directing the lead of the higher ranking of the other two plain suits, the spade suit. When West took the ◇ Q with his ace, he read the ◇ 8 as a suit-preference signal. He knew this eightspot was from ◇ 8-5-4-2, as the deuce had been played on the opening ◇ K lead as a discouraging signal. With a knowing smile, West led a spade to his partner's ♠ A that broke the contract. Declarer was caught stealing and got a bottom score. The next time South will not bid to reach the moon, especially against these opponents.

Grand larceny pays off at the bridge table if you can get away with it; but before you attempt it, select your customers with care.

On the next deal a defender flaunts his wealth by throwing a king on declarer's ace. He was not unblocking, he was signalling for the winning play.

Deal 15 Majestic Mien

♠ K J
♡ 10 8 4
◇ A 10 5 4
♣ J 5 4 2

♠ A 7
♡ K J 9 6 3 2
◇ 8 2
♣ 8 7 3

♠ 9 8 6 5 4 2
♡ Q 7
◇ K 3
♣ 10 9 6

♠ Q 10 3
♡ A 5
◇ Q J 9 7 6
♣ A K Q

South opened 1 NT, North said 2 NT; and South 3 NT, end.

West opened the ♡ 6 to East's queen that won because declarer held up the ♡ A. East returned the ♡ 7 to ace, and West followed suit with the KING of hearts in majestic mien. This king throwaway struck East like a ton of bricks. The ♡ K play could only be construed as a suit-preference signal for a higher-ranking suit. Dummy showed the ◇ A, so a spade lead was indicated.

Hoping for the best, declarer finessed the ◇ Q, losing to king. East, no longer on a guess, returned a spade to West's ace. West ran his hearts to defeat the contract three tricks.

In the next deal East and West were playing the weak notrump on 12 to 14 points. This bid is a good match-point tactic but is treacherous at rubber bridge, especially against strong opponents. North and South were hard pressed and they failed to reach their best contract, 3 NT. Yet the actual 4 ♠ contract could have been made, were it not for the direction afforded by a suit-preference signal.

Deal 16 Back To Orbit

West	North	East
	♠ K J 10 3 ♡ A J 8 ◇ Q J 9 7 ♣ A 10	
♠ A 5 ♡ Q 6 5 ◇ A K 8 4 2 ♣ J 6 3		♠ 6 4 ♡ 10 9 3 2 ◇ 3 ♣ 9 8 7 5 4 2
	♠ Q 9 8 7 2 ♡ K 7 4 ◇ 10 6 5 ♣ K Q	

West	North	East	South
1 NT	Double	3 ♣!	3 ♠
Pass	4 ♠ (final bid)		

West opened the ◇ K. The fall of East's ◇ 3 and

South's ◇ 10 false card were discouraging. Whom was West to believe? Not daring to risk another diamond lead, West switched to a club which dummy's ♣ A won. East followed suit with the ♣ 2 which West read as suit preference, asking for a diamond lead presumably to ruff it.

West, no slouch at the bridge table, caught the inference. Against North's takeout double,* East's 3 ♣ bid was marked as a pre-empt on a long suit of rags in clubs.

Next declarer led dummy's ♠ J, losing to West's ♠ A. West, now knowing the lay of the diamond suit, thanks to his partner's SPS, went back into orbit. West cashed the ◇ A and noted partner's discard of the ♣ 4, a repeat SPS that confirmed the presence of a trump still left in East's hand which could serve to ruff a diamond. So West led another diamond to let East ruff for the setting trick.

While suit-preference signals give defenders an edge over declarer in some situations, it would be under-rating declarer to think that he would not try to set up a counter defense. In the next deal both declarer and defenders received par for their superb play. Hands like this make bridge fascinating.

---

*Actually aimed at penalties had East passed, and South would also pass 1 NT unless holding less than 7 high-card points. **Editor.**

Deal 17 Tit For Tat

West	North	East
	♠ 7 6 5 4	
	♡ A K Q J	
	◇ 10 6	
	♣ Q J 7	
♠ K 3 2		♠ 8
♡ 3		♡ 9 7 6 5 4 2
◇ A Q J 7 5 4		◇ K 3 2
♣ 10 9 4		♣ 6 5 2
	♠ A Q J 10 9	
	♡ 10 8	
	◇ 9 8	
	♣ A K 8 3	

South	West	North	East
1 ♠	2 ◇	4 ♠	(final bid)

West opened his ♡ 3 to jack in dummy and East followed with the NINE of hearts.

This unnecessarily high card was recognized as a SPS directing the lead of the higher-ranking of the other two plain suits, a diamond. It was self-evident that the opening lead was a singleton and that West hoped to make good use of his trumps.

To declarer this was as plain as the nose on his face. Spurning the finesse, declarer led a trump off dummy and came up with the ace, then led the nine. Figuring that declarer was playing for a 2 — 2 trump split, West won the second trump lead with his king. This would reserve a trump for a possible ruff. On this trick West saw his partner discard his lowest club, the deuce. This was a discard suit-preference signal, confirming East's previous SPS calling for a diamond lead.

West, trying to picture his partner's hand, figured that with a single spade and four diamonds, East would probably have sacrified at 5 ♢. The negative inference was that East held at least two.

West led his ♢ A and East dropped the trey. Were it not for East's ♡ 9 play and ♣ 2 discard, West would have been disillusioned. So West led the ♢ 7 that East won with the king and East returned a heart which West ruffed for the setting trick.

Actually the above play was a pipe dream. Of course West opened the ♡ 3 and East played the ♡ 9. From then on both defenders were due for a rude awakening.

Declarer was a wily old fox who knew his way around bridge tables. The ♡ 3 lead carried an evil omen. This and East's ♡ 9 play, which South recognized as a SPS for a diamond lead, caused South to look for a counter attack. So he concocted a plan to hold his loss to three tricks, and the percentage favoring it made to look attractive.

Rejecting the hope for a 2 — 2 trump split, declarer led a trump to the ace. Next he pushed three rounds of clubs, and as he had hoped, both defenders followed suit. Declarer led his fourth club and cared not which trump either defender used to ruff it. When

West ruffed with the ♠ 3, declarer had a choice of two winning plays. He could discard a diamond from dummy, or overruff West. Declarer spread his hand, and announced that the contract was in the bag and his total loss was three tricks.

In many commonplace situations, a defender can express suit preference when following suit on a trick won by declarer. In the next deal the possibility of setting the contract is based on wishful thinking. But if the only way to defeat a contract is if your partner has certain cards, wishful thinking is proper.

Deal 18, 4 ♡ by South — Lavinthal Twice

West	North	East
	♠ 8 7 2 ♡ J 8 5 4 3 ◇ K 10 ♣ Q 7 3	
♠ J 10 9 6 3 ♡ 7 ◇ A Q 3 ♣ J 9 8 2		♠ A 4 ♡ A 2 ◇ J 8 7 6 5 ♣ 10 6 5 4
	♠ K Q 5 ♡ K Q 10 9 6 ◇ 9 4 2 ♣ A K	

South opened 1 ♡, North bid 2 ♡, and S 4 ♡, end.

West opened the ♠ J and East's ace won the trick. East returned his last spade to declarer's king and

West, knowing that East had no spade left, played the TEN OF SPADES. West's unnecessarily high spade play directed the lead of the higher ranking of the two remaining suits, in this case a diamond.

Declarer led the nine of trumps to East's ace. East could clearly read the message that rode on his partner's ♠ 10 play. Only if it was a forced play could this card be read as carrying no message.* After a review of the auction, East quickly dismissed this possibility. Hence it became crystal clear that West wanted a diamond lead.

East elected to lead the ◇ J. With the ◇ 10 visible in dummy, the story told was, "I still hold a trump and I hope to ruff a spade."

West won the ◇ J with the ◇ A and switched to a spade which his partner ruffed. This defeated the contract.

Without the first SPS (♠ 10 play), East could have misguessed and led a club to trick four. This would be more likely than the diamond lead. With a club lead the spade ruff would be lost. Declarer would pat himself on the back because, while he and his partner used SPS, his opponents still lived in an ivory tower.

Of course, the second SPS (◇ J lead) might not

---

*If West held ♠ J-10 dry, declarer would have held a five-card spade suit which he would most probably have bid. **Editor.**

have been necessary because simple logic would have dictated a spade return to trick four. Let us call it insurance, lest West get ideas about returning a club, instead of a spade which East could ruff.

On the next deal normal signals complemented by suit preference signals set up a chain reaction which tumbled the roof down on declarer. It only goes to prove that it takes more than aces and kings to set a contract.

Little did West realize that his apparently worthless hand would key declarer's downfall.

Deal 19 — Chain Reaction

North:
♠ Q 7
♡ Q 10 9 7
◇ K Q J 7 4
♣ K Q

West:
♠ J 10 5 3 2
♣ 5 2
◇ —
♣ 10 9 5 4 3 2

East:
♠ A K
♡ K J
◇ 9 8 6 5 3
♣ J 8 7 6

South:
♠ 9 8 6 4
♡ A 8 6 4 3
◇ A 10 2
♣ A

West	North	East	South
Pass	1 ◇	Pass	1 ♡
Pass	2 ♡	Pass	4 ♡
Pass	Pass	Pass	

West opened the ♠ 3 and East played the ♠ A, then ♠ K.

Declarer, with aces topping the other three suits, smiled serenely, not knowing that a storm was brewing. West, reading his partner to be dry of spades, awoke with a start. He saw a chance to set the contract. On the ♠ K West played the JACK of spades, a SPS directing the lead of the higher ranking of the other two plain suits, a diamond. Both declarer and East recognized West's intent on the ♠ J play. Declarer's smile withered. Posed with no guess, East led a diamond which West ruffed.

West returned an unnecessarily high spade, the TEN, to show ability to ruff another diamond. Dummy trumped high with the ♡ Q and East overruffed with the ♡ K.

Declarer wondered when this crossruff would end. Seeking another spade lead, East led his ◇ 9 and again West ruffed. In compliance with this SPS, the unnecessarily high ◇ 9, West returned another spade. Again dummy trumped high with the ♡ 10 and East overruffed with the ♡ J, setting declarer three tricks.

If East guesses wrong and leads a club to trick three, declarer is safe. Declarer leads the ♡ A then a low heart to draw trumps.

2. LEAD SUIT-PREFERENCE SIGNALS

This species comprises leads made to direct partner to return another specified suit. Typical are the incidental ♠ 10 and ♢ 9 leads in the previous deal. Yet it belongs in Species 1 because the first and vital signal, West's ♠ J, was a follow-suit SPS.

Ruffing positions occur often and a simple suit-preference signal tells partner how to take advantage of them. The next hand I sent to the late Louis H. Watson soon after his great book, *Watson on the Play of the Hand,* was published in 1934.* This example he used in his daily newspaper column, where he hailed this new defense weapon.

---

*A more modern textbook is "The Play of the Cards" by Fred Karpin, Bridge Quarterly 1958. In our opinion you will find this book a worthwhile addition to your bridge library. (Out of print.) **Editor.**

Deal 20 Entry For Ruff

♠ K 4
♡ K Q J 3
◇ 7 4 2
♣ K 8 6 3

♠ A 7 2
♡ 9 8
◇ A Q 9 8 6 3
♣ J 2

♠ J 9 6 5 3
♡ 6 5
◇ J
♣ 10 9 7 5 4

♠ Q 10 8
♡ A 10 7 4 2
◇ K 10 5
♣ A Q

South	West	North	East
1 ♡	2 ◇	3 ♡	Pass
4 ♡	Pass	Pass	Pass

Opening leads are not a cut and dried proposition and West had a problem. He led the ◇ A, as good as anything. He hoped to find the king or singleton in partner's hand. When the ◇ J did fall from East, prospects of breaking the contract brightened. West next led the ◇ 9 which East ruffed. East pondered on that ◇ 9 lead. This unnecessarily high card must be suit preference, directing East to return the higher ranking of the other two plain suits, a spade. So East led a spade to West's ace and East ruffed another diamond to set the contract.

Without the SPS, which suit should East return

to trick three? It would be a sheer guess. If East guesses wrong and returns a club, declarer takes it, draws trumps, and scores game.

Ruffing positions like this provide frequent opportunities for SPS's. In many cases a defender opens a singleton which his partner wins. This partner, wanting the lower ranking of the other two plain suits led back, returns his LOWEST card of the same suit. Likewise the return lead of an UNNECESSARILY HIGH CARD directs the higher ranking of the other two plain suits. It is simple and effective.

Below we see how a review of the bidding can set the stage for a suit-preference signal. Such a situation occurs often, but many players miss the opportunity because they are not alert.

Deal 21, Love All — Inferential Countdown

	North	
	♠ 10 9 6 5 3	
	♡ K 8 7	
	◇ K 8 4	
	♣ 9 8	
♠ A J		♠ 7
♡ 10 6 5		♡ A Q J 9
◇ 10 7 5 3		◇ 9 2
♣ K 10 6 5		♣ A Q J 7 4 2
	♠ K Q 8 4 2	
	♡ 4 3 2	
	◇ A Q J 6	
	♣ 3	

West	North	East	South
——	——	1 ♣	1 ♠
2 ♣	2 ♠	4 ♣	4 ♠
Double	Pass	Pass	Pass

For East — West 5 ♣ is cold, but West felt dubious and preferred to double 4 ♠ for a sure reward. In a duplicate game five aggressive pairs did bid 5 ♣ and scored 400 points.

At 4 ♠ doubled West opened the ♣ 5 to East's ace. For an instant, East was in a quandary as to his next lead. A review of the auction cleared the air. West's club raise must be based on four clubs, standard practice for supporting what could be a short club opening. Seeing no alternative, East led the QUEEN of clubs, an unnecessarily high card implying suit preference. Declarer ruffed as expected.

West pondered, " My partner led his highest club, knowing that declarer would ruff. Why?" The ♣ Q can not win a trick, therefore it directed West to lead the higher ranking of the other two plain suits, a heart. Declarer lost the ♠ K to West's ace. West led the ♡ 10 as a forcing card. After East won the third heart trick, he pushed his fourth heart, hoping to promote a trump trick for West. This en passant play did so, scoring the third setting trick and netting 500 points for a top score.

Without the SPS, West at trick four could misguess and return a diamond, letting declarer get nine tricks for down one, a good score for South.

If West inconveniently opens the ♣ K to see dummy and to hold the lead, East should play the ♣ Q to ask for a heart shift. This West could read as a SPS because East must hold six clubs for his jump rebid of 4 ♣ and so South will ruff the second club lead. So West should shift to the ♡ 10.

Like detectives Dr. Watson and Sherlock Holmes, two snoopers made a primary signal, then a suit-preference signal to track declarer DOWN!

Deal 22 Goren's Delight

North:
♠ A K Q 9
♡ A 8 4 2
♢ 9 8 5 2
♣ 10

West:
♠ —
♡ J 10 3
♢ A K 10 7 3
♣ K J 8 7 2

East:
♠ 10 8 7 6 5 3
♡ Q 5
♢ Q J
♣ 5 4 3

South:
♠ J 4 2
♡ K 9 7 6
♢ 6 4
♣ A Q 9 6

West	North	East	South
1 ♢	Double	Pass	2 ♡
Pass	4 ♡	(final bid)	

West opened the ◇ K and he saw the queen drop from his partner's hand. Either the queen was dry or it was a primary signal from queen-jack. Either way, it was safe for West to lead away from his ace. To trick two West gave East a gainful inference by leading the TEN of diamonds to East's jack. East noted the unnecessarily high diamond, the ten, and he read it as suit preference for a lead in the higher ranking of the other two plain suits, a spade. So East dutifully returned a spade; and please note the PARTICULAR SPADE, THE TEN. East knew that West would read it as an irregular lead with the ♠ 9 showing in dummy. West ruffed the ♠ 10 and he in turn looked for the motive behind the irregular ♠ 10 lead. Did East want another diamond lead? West knew that both East and declarer had no diamond left. The only gain by a diamond lead now would be an uppercut by a high trump.

So West returned the ◇ 7 to dummy's ◇ 8, East trumped high with the ♡ Q, and declarer overruffed with the ♡ K. This uppercut play promoted a natural trump trick for West's ♡ J-10 for the setting trick. Despite defeat, South complimented his opponents for their superb defense.

The term, uppercut, was coined by Charles H. Goren to describe a defensive (usually) trump promotion play like East's trumping with the ♡ Q. The French verb "couper" means to cut, strike or blow; and the

French use the word in bridge to mean to trump or to ruff. Goren aptly added the pugilistic touch to describe accurately and delightfully this particular play.

In the next deal you can beat 4 ♡ at double dummy. Yet how can defenders defeat 4 ♡ on the rub of the green? Playing East, how can you direct a diamond lead to your ace? Playing West, how can you signal for continued club leads? Are suit-preference signals indispensable?

Deal 23 A Noble Nine

West	North	East
	♠ K 6 2	
	♡ 5	
	◇ Q 8 4 3	
	♣ 7 5 4 3 2	
♠ 9 8 5 4 3		♠ Q 7
♡ A 9 4		♡ 6 2
◇ J 9 7 2		◇ A 10 5
♣ Q		♣ A K J 10 9 6
	♠ A J 10	
	♡ K Q J 10 8 7 3	
	◇ K 6	
	♣ 8	

East opened 1 ♣, South jumped to 4 ♡, West doubled and all passed.

West opened the ♣ Q, which East overtook with his king. To East the best defense looked like high club leads to promote trumps for partner.

To trick two East led the NINE of clubs, readable as the LOWEST master club that he could spare. West read this as a SPS, directing the lead of the lower ranking of the other two plain suits, a diamond. Declarer trumped the ♣ 9 with the ♡ K and West properly refrained from overruffing with his ace. Instead West discarded the ♠ 3, obviously his lowest spade with the deuce visible in dummy. This East read as an SPS, directing the lead of the lower ranking of West's OTHER two plain suits.* What could be clearer? West wanted his partner to push clubs at every chance. West could have told the same story by discarding the ◇ 2, but he did not wish to unguard ◇ J-9-7-2. Later on the diamond stopper could be critical.

To trick three South led the ♡ 10 which West won with his ace. West returned a diamond to East's ace, and East pushed another club, promoting *en passant* West's noble nine of trumps to a winner that broke the contract.

Without using SPS's, West to trick four could guess wrong and lead a spade, ending declarer's problems.

If East held the ♠ A instead of the ◇ A, his SPS in clubs would be the ace, then king.

---

*A discard suit-preference signal. See Section 3 on Species 3 SPS's. **Editor.**

The next deal illustrates how a recognizable unconventional lead laid the groundwork for the killing defensive play. The unorthodox lead coaxed a suit-preference signal from the partner and declarer did not have a chance.

Deal 24 King Fifth

North:
♠ 8 7 4 3 2
♡ 8 5
◇ K 8
♣ A Q 7 5

West:
♠ 10 6
♡ K 9 6 4 2
◇ 10 9 3 2
♣ 9 3

East:
♠ A
♡ A Q J 7 3
◇ 7 6 4
♣ K J 10 2

South:
♠ K Q J 9 5
♡ 10
◇ A Q J 5
♣ 8 6 4

West	North	East	South
——	——	1 ♡*	1 ♠
Pass	2 ♠	Double	3 ♠
4 ♡	4 ♠	(final bid)	

Before leading, West put on his thinking cap.

*"Do not open four-card majors" was checked on East's convention card.

His entryless hand germed a brilliant idea. Perhaps East needs a lead through dummy in a minor suit. So West opened his ♡ K from king fifth instead of his fourth best to HOLD THE LEAD. This unusual card coupled with the auction indicated to East that the ♡ K probably headed a five timer so that the defense could get at most one trick from hearts. So East played the ♡ 3, his lowest heart, as a SPS for a club switch.

West read this SPS, for East would not open a four-card heart suit and declarer was marked with a singleton heart. West shifted to the ♣ 9, and declarer won with dummy's ace, knowing that the queen finesse would lose. Declarer lost a spade to East's ace, and East cashed his ♣ K, seeing West complete his plain ♣ 3 echo. Finally East led a third club that West ruffed for the setting trick.

Annoyed at going down, North asked South, "Before leading trumps, why don't you run four diamonds to get two club discards from dummy?" This proved futile, for East ruffs the fourth diamond with the ♠ A, cashes his ♣ K, then leads a third club to let West score his trump ten.

If West opens his fourth-best heart, East is endplayed at once. Many textbooks overlook an important principle here. If you are poor in entries and hold many low cards to the king in partner's bid suit, lead your king rather than your fourth best.

The next deal illustrates a unique application of suit preference. A defender with a winner forced his partner to ruff a loser for the evident purpose of directing a lead in a specific suit.

Deal 25 Passing The Buck

West	North	East
	♠ Q 7 4 3 ♡ J 6 2 ◇ K 8 5 4 ♣ K 6	
♠ 6 5 2 ♡ 10 4 ◇ 10 3 2 ♣ 9 7 5 4 2		♠ A ♡ A Q 9 8 3 ◇ 9 7 6 ♣ A Q J 8
	♠ K J 10 9 8 ♡ K 7 5 ◇ A Q J ♣ 10 3	

West	North	East	South
Pass	Pass	1 ♡	1 ♠
Pass	2 ♠	Double	3 ♠
Pass	Pass	Pass	

West opened the ♡ 10, dummy ducked, East signalled with the nine, and declarer won with the king. Declarer led the ♠ J to East's dry ace. East cashed the ♡ Q, so obviously held the ♡ A also. When East saw his partner drop the ♡ 4 with the ♡ 3 and ♡ 2 visible, he knew West was out of hearts.

East *deliberately* led the ♡ Q rather than the ♡ A to set the stage for the lead of a LOW heart in case West held fewer than three hearts.

The plot that East hatched was unfolding. East led the ♡ 3, forcing his partner to ruff. West read his partner's purpose of passing the buck rather than cashing the ♡ A. West read East's lowest heart lead as a suit-preference signal, directing the lead of the lower ranking of the other two plain suits, a club. So West returned a club which let East win two club tricks and set declarer one trick.

If East wanted a diamond return, he would have led the ♡ 8 instead of the ♡ 3, an unnecessarily high card asking for a diamond lead.

If East plays both his top hearts to tricks three and four, he has no chance to win two club tricks, — unless West has the perspicacity to ruff the third heart and the voodoo insight to return a club instead of a diamond, a sheer guess.

Without using SPS's, East can lead low on his third heart lead to force West to ruff; but this superior plan leaves West in need of the services of a voodoo doctor to find the winning club return.

The next deal from a duplicate game illustrates the thought processes of a pair of top-flight defenders.

Deal 26, E-W vul. Grand Rush

North:
♠ A Q J 7 4
♡ 10 7 6 2
◇ A Q
♣ K 4

West:
♠ 9 8 6 5 2
♡ A 4 3
◇ J 8 2
♣ 6 3

East:
♠ ——
♡ 8
◇ 9 7 6 4 3
♣ A Q J 10 8 7 5

South:
♠ K 10 3
♡ K Q J 9 5
◇ K 10 5
♣ 9 2

West	North	East	South
——	1 ♠	3 ♣*	3 ♡
Pass	4 ♡	(final bid)	

West opened the ♣ 6 to king and ace. East paused to canvass his chances of setting the contract. Clearly a diamond or a trump lead promised no nourishment. But a fast entry to the hand of his partner, before trumps were drawn, who would lead a spade for a ruff,

*Weak jump overcall, today a popular tactic.

looked like the only chance for the setting trick. This was a long shot, yet worth a try. This fast entry, had to be the ace of trumps and it had to be scored without drawing East's lone trump. All this was wishful thinking, but it paid dividends.

East won trick two with the ♣ Q, then he led the Jack of clubs. *West saw that East held all the remaining clubs and that East could have led any one of the other clubs with equal effect on declarer's play.* So the ♣ J lead contained the implication of a suit preference. The ♣ Q then ♣ J leads, both unnecessarily high cards, lent double emphasis on the urgent need of a lead in the higher ranking of the other two plain suits, in this case a spade.

On the ♣ J lead, declarer discarded a low diamond and West huddled. West recognized the SPS for a spade lead and its urgency must be foremost, for his partner had voluntarily given declarer a ruff and discard. Recognizing that time was of the essence, West hopped up with his ace of trumps and returned a spade.

This East ruffed with his lone trump, upsetting declarer's applecart with one grand rush.

To achieve maximum results with suit-preference and other signals, it is important for each defender to use the best technique in exploiting a ruffing position. The trick gained is only exchanged if the suit led for a ruff lets declarer discard a loser on a loser. Stop and think before each lead.

Deal 27 A Fast Cash

North:
♠ 8 6 3
♡ K 7 5 3
◇ K Q 7 2
♣ Q 5

West:
♠ J 4
♡ 10 8 6 2
◇ 3
♣ J 8 7 6 4 3

East:
♠ Q 5
♡ A Q 9
◇ A J 10 9 5 4
♣ 10 2

South:
♠ A K 10 9 7 2
♡ J 4
◇ 8 6
♣ A K 9

South	West	North	East
1 ♠	Pass	1 NT	2 ◇
2 ♠	Pass	3 ♠	(final bid)

West opened the ◇ 3, clearly a sneak from East's view. Dummy's queen lost to East's ace. To promote dimond ruffs to the utmost, East led the ◇ J, an unnecessarily high card, directing his partner to lead the higher ranking of the other two plain suits, a heart. So West ruffed the ◇ J and returned the ♡ 2. Dummy ducked so East's queen won. As the ♡ 2 looked like West's fourth best, East counted declarer for holding one more heart, probably the jack as dummy had played low.

If East unthinkingly now leads a diamond, it does promote a natural defense trick in trumps, but it would let declarer discard a loser on a loser, his ♡ J. East wisely refrained from an immediate diamond lead. Instead, like little old ladies who "quickly their aces take lest they do not make," *East first made a fast cash of his ♡ A, then led a diamond.* Declarer, caught between two millstones in this *en passant sec* position, inserted the ♠ 9, hoping for the miracle of finding ♠ Q-J with East. But West overruffed to set declarer one trick.

If instead declarer ruffs with a top trump, the defense comes to a natural trump trick.

Declarer was not so downcast over the disaster because it gave him a chance to pun his partner. "Ruff going against these opponents," he remarked as they moved to the next table.

With a good partnership, negative inferences play a part almost equal to positive ones. In the next deal East's 2 ◇ bid gave West a clue that decided the course of the defense. This, plus a suit-preference signal, sealed the fate of declarer.

Deal 28 Three Clues

West		North		East
		♠ A K J 5		
		♡ K 7 3		
		◇ K 9 3		
		♣ K 9 2		
♠ 7				♠ 6 2
♡ A Q 10 6 5 4				♡ 2
◇ A J 4				◇ Q 10 8 6 5 2
♣ Q 8 4				♣ 7 6 5 3
		♠ Q 10 9 8 4 3		
		♡ J 9 8		
		◇ 7		
		♣ A J 10		

West	North	East	South
1 ♡	Double	2 ◇	3 ♠!
Pass	4 ♠	(final bid)	

Before making the opening lead, West reviewed the bidding. His partner's 2 ◇ bid offered a clue. Knowing that probably his partner would not run out against a takeout double with two or more hearts, West opened the ♡ A. He noted his partner's ♡ 2 and read it as probably a singleton. So next West led the TEN of hearts, declarer played low from dummy, and East ruffed. East read partner's ♡ 10 lead as a SPS, calling for the lead of the higher ranking of the two other plain suits, a diamond. So East returned a diamond, and note East's choice, the TEN. With the ◇ 9 visible in dummy, the ◇ 10 lead could be read as a SPS. It confirmed another trump with East, with which he hoped to ruff another heart. West took the ◇ 10 with his ace, and returned another heart to let East ruff and for the setting trick.

Three clues keyed the winning defense. If East was partnered with one who could not read beyond his nose, the ♡ 2 would have been read as a discouraging signal. And if West had shifted to any other suit at trick two, declarer would have had a good play for his contract.

Clues number two and three, of course, were the two SPS's that directed the right leads. Without these right leads, even if one link in the chain of three clues fails, declarer can get home with ten tricks.

3. DISCARD SUIT-PREFERENCE SIGNALS*

A discard is defined as the play of a card which is not of the suit led and not a trump.** When you play a card of another suit on the suit led, the natural inference is that you have no card of the suit led. When playing primary signals you have three specific ways of discarding.

First is the encouraging discard, usually a seven or higher card from your best suit to alert partner to lead it. Later a second discard of lower rank from the same suit will complete the echo and confirm the strength in that suit.

The second way is like the first, except that the first discard is so low that partner will have difficulty reading it as the start of an echo. For example, discarding the ◇ 5 from ◇ A-K-5-3-2 will not excite partner until later he sees you drop the deuce to complete the echo.

When you are unable to discard safely by either method described above, you can resort to a third method of signalling partner. You first discard the lowest card from one suit and on your next chance you discard the lowest card from another suit. The negative inference is that you have a trick in the third suit,

---

*Sometimes called off-suit discards. **Editor.**

****Despite this standard definition it is possible to discard a low trump after an opponent has ruffed high. Editor.**

yet this may be only a possible trick. You may have to guard such a third suit as ◇ 10-7-4-3 against a ◇ A-K-Q-2 in dummy. While no trick is in view for you, you must keep all this suit lest dummy's ◇ 2 score the fourth trick against you. One inherent deficiency of this two-suit echo is that if your partner gets in before you make your second discard, he must guess which remaining suit you want led.

LAVINTHAL DISCARD

Each method above has defects which were accepted as necessary evils because nothing better was proposed. The method which I advocate needs ONLY ONE DISCARD TO DIRECT A LEAD IN A SPECIFIC SUIT. It is simple. When void of one suit, you have three suits left. To pinpoint a specific suit, your FIRST HIGH OR LOWEST DISCARD from another suit tells partner which suit you want led. When left with three suits, you have the suit you want led and two other suits. YOU HAVE A CHOICE OF TWO SUITS FROM WHICH TO MAKE ONE DISCARD WHICH WILL PINPOINT THE THIRD SUIT. For example, you are unable to follow suit in spades and you want to direct a heart lead. A high diamond discard will tell your partner that you want led the higher-ranking of the other two remaining suits. A high club discard will likewise give the same message, — LEAD HEARTS. Or perhaps you are unable to follow suit on hearts and you want a diamond led. A high spade discard will ask partner to lead the higher-ranking of the other two suits. If you can better afford a club discard, your lowest club will also ask for a diamond lead. What could be simpler?

By adopting the Lavinthal Discard you gain greater flexibility. You also have the negative inference that no likely trick lies in the suit from which you make your first discard. However, nothing will prevent you from making a low or high discard, if it will serve your purpose better, from such a suit as ♡ K-8-2 over ♡ A-x-x in dummy.

By the Lavinthal Discard Suit-Preference Signal, you are able to direct the lead of a suit of all busy cards that cannot withstand a primary discard. It might be ◇ K-9 (doubleton) over ◇ A-Q-x in dummy, or the Q-J-3, the A-J-9, or perhaps the A-K-Q-J of a suit at notrump where a discard would cost a trick.

The Discard SPS, unlike other SPS's, cannot be used simultaneouly with primary discards. They are incompatible. Defenders must agree to abandon primary discards to gain the advantage of the newer type of defensive weapon.

Because the advantages of the discard suit-preference signal are so evident, I urge that you and your partner adopt it as standard procedure. If used in tournaments, on your convention card you list "Lavinthal Discards," or "Off-Suit Discards."

Albert H. Morehead, bridge editor of the *New York Times,* in 1935 reported the next deal. The rebid of two notrump by opener was optimistic by present-day standards, yet such thin rebids are still made in many bridge circles.

Deal 29 Basic Discard

West	North	East
	♠ K 8 3	
	♡ 10 5 4	
	◇ Q 9	
	♣ A Q 7 5 4	
♠ 10 6 4		♠ J 9 7 5 2
♡ K 7 2		♡ A Q J 9
◇ K 6		◇ 8 5 4 2
♣ J 10 9 8 2		♣ —
	♠ A Q	
	♡ 8 6 3	
	◇ A J 10 7 3	
	♣ K 6 3	

South	West	North	East
1 ◇	Pass	2 ♣	Pass
2 NT (?)	Pass	3 NT (final bid)	

West opened the ♣ J, dummy's queen held, and East discarded the TWO of diamonds. West read this basic discard as a suit-preference signal, designating the lead of the lower ranking of the two remaining suits, a heart. Declarer, needing to set up the diamond suit for contract, finessed the ♢ Q to West's ♢ K. Complying with his partner's suit-preference discard, West switched to a heart and the defenders garnered four heart tricks to set the contract.

Defenders have much to gain if they change over to the use of suit-preference discards. Their simplicity and effectiveness are apparent.

Note that if East's first discard was an unnecessarily high spade, the nine, it would have sent the same message. "Lead the higher ranking of the other two suits, a heart."

Using primary discards, East could not discard the ♡ 9 without sacrificing a critical trick. To avoid this, East would have to pinpoint the heart suit piecemeal fashion. First East discards his bottom diamond then at his first opportunity his bottom spade, or vice versa. As it happens, East would not be able to make his second discard in time to take his partner off a guess. West may be reluctant to lead away from his ♡ K and he would play safely by persisting with a second club lead.

In suit-preference discards, the first discard of the lowest card or of an unnecessarily high card amounts to a command to lead the suit designated.

At times a defender opens a suit against a notrump contract and soon finds out that his suit is a lost cause. The partner of the opening leader may not be aware of the futility of working on the opening leader's suit. The next deal shows how a defender can send a double message, — to abandon the original suit and to shift to another SPECIFIC suit.

Deal 30 Double Message

West	North	East
	♠ 6 3	
	♡ 9 5	
	◇ 8 4	
	♣ A K 10 9 7 3 2	
♠ 9 5 4 2		♠ Q J 10 7
♡ A 10 8 6		♡ Q J 3 2
◇ J 10 6 5 2		◇ K 7
♣ ——		♣ Q 5 4
	♠ A K 8	
	♡ K 7 4	
	◇ A Q 9 3	
	♣ J 8 6	

South opened 1 NT and North made it 3 NT.

West opened the ◇ 5, which went to the king and the ace. Declarer led the ♣ J and West saw his chance to warn his partner by a two-fold message. On this lead West discarded the ◇ 2 showing that diamonds were a mad quest, and because his discard was the lowest card, it directed a heart shift. East, in with the ♣ Q, read his partner's suit-preference signal and shifted to the ♡ Q. Declarer's ♡ K was trapped and declarer was set one trick.

If instead West prefers a spade lead rather than a heart, he would discard the ◇ J, still holding diamond control and asking for a spade shift by partner.

If West has nothing worthwhile in either major suit or in diamonds, he would discard a middle diamond, the six. This would advise, "Partner, you are on your own. Use your judgement."

If not using SPS's, West would discard a diamond to ask for a switch. Without the SPS clues, East would switch to a spade, his superior suit. Of course, the ♡ 8 discard would be more specific because it would direct a heart lead. However, hearts would block if declarer takes the right view and holds up his ♡ K until the third heart lead.

After the ♡ 8 discard, declarer would place only three hearts left with West, for with five or more West would have opened a heart instead of a diamond. So ducking twice in hearts insures the 3 NT contract, — unless East is canny enough to push the queen then jack from ♡ A-Q-J-x and declarer twice holds up the ♡ K.

The usual function of a suit-preference signal is to direct a shift to one of the other plain suits. However, when the necessity arises, the SPS is so versatile that a partner can be directed to continue leading his originally-led suit. The next deal shows how simple this is.

Deal 31 *En Passant*

	North	
	♠ 8 6 5 3	
	♡ J 4 2	
	◇ K 4	
	♣ A Q J 2	
West		**East**
♠ Q 9		♠ 7 4
♡ A 10 9 8 7		♡ 6 5
◇ 3		◇ A Q J 10 9 7 5 2
♣ 10 9 8 6 3		♣ 7
	South	
	♠ A K J 10 2	
	♡ K Q 3	
	◇ 8 6	
	♣ K 5 4	

South	West	North	East
1 ♠	Pass	2 ♣	3 ◇
3 ♠	Pass	4 ♠	(final bid)

West led the ◇ 3 that went to the king and the ace. Next East cashed his queen on which West discarded the ♣ 3, obviously his bottom club with the deuce visible in dummy. West knew that a SPS directs attention to a suit other than the suit where the SPS was made, — in this case the lead of the lower ranking of the other two plain suits.

Thought East, "What could be clearer? My partner wants me to push a third diamond. Lucky me. I was about to switch to a heart."

So East deferred to his partner and led a third diamond. This *en passant* play promoted a natural trump trick from West's ♠ Q-9, to be made now or later depending on how high declarer trumped.

Usually, offering declarer a ruff and a sluff is a crime play that costs a trick. But here one heart discard from declarer's hand or from dummy was not enough to prevent West from later scoring his ♡ A for the setting trick.

A careless West might have played a HIGH club to trick two as a suit preference for a heart lead. But our West defender was discerning. He knew that his ♡ A was a trick that he would be fairly sure to get anyway and that it could wait upon the urgent chance to promote a trump trick. This kind of play scores tops in duplicate games.

How can you make sure that your partner will stay in orbit and follow through with his original objective, leading the same suit after your brilliant play? In the deal below, defense was a cinch due to suit preference.

Deal 32 Stay In Orbit

West	North	East
	♠ K 9 5	
	♡ 6	
	◇ K J 10 9 4	
	♣ Q 7 3 2	
♠ Q 8 4 2		♠ 10 7 3
♡ J 9 7 3 2		♡ A Q 5
◇ A 6 5		◇ 8 7
♣ 9		♣ J 10 8 6 4
	♠ A J 6	
	♡ K 10 8 4	
	◇ Q 3 2	
	♣ A K 5	

South opened 1 NT, North said 2 NT; and South with a bit extra over his 16 points bid 3 NT.

West opened the ♡ 3 and East played his QUEEN. This queen play is a standard tactic of good players to frighten declarer into taking his ♡ K at once if he has it, lest "the rats get at it" and big brother rat in West knock it off with the ace on the return lead.

South, duly intimidated, won his ♡ K, hoping that his ♡ 10 would secure another trick later.

Declarer attacked diamonds and West held up his ace until the third round. This holdup was aimed at giving East the utmost freedom to signal. On West's ◇ A, East dropped his lowest club, the four, emphatically confirming heart strength.

West, although disheartened with his weak heart suit, stayed in orbit and led another low heart to East's ace. East returned his last heart to let West pick up South's guarded ten. When the battle was over, declarer had lost the ◇ A and four heart tricks, — down one.

If declarer holds up his ♡ K, he still loses four heart tricks and the ◇ A, going down one.

If you sat East, how could you assure your partner that you held the key heart card without using SPS's? Confining yourself to primary signals, you would have to hope that your partner would stay in orbit with his hearts and not panic by leading a black suit.

Using primary discards a defender is sometimes unable to complete the message that would guarantee a specific lead. In the next deal from a duplicate game, some defenders overcame this handicap by use of the Lavinthal Discard Suit-Preference Signal.

Deal 33 Looking For Data

North:
♠ 7 5 4 3
♡ K J
◇ A Q 10 5
♣ K J 10

West:
♠ A K
♡ 10 9 5 4 3
◇ 6 4 3
♣ 9 8 6

East:
♠ 9
♡ Q 8 7 6 2
◇ J 9 7
♣ A Q 3 2

South:
♠ Q J 10 8 6 2
♡ A
◇ K 8 2
♣ 7 5 4

West	North	East	South
——	1 ♣	Pass	1 ♠
Pass	2 ♠	Pass	4 ♠
Pass	Pass	Pass	

At nearly all tables West led the ♠ A then ♠ K, hoping that his partner would show out and with his discard would give a message to clarify the subsequent defense.

Where the SPS was not used, East was hard put to find a good informative discard. The lowest heart would suggest a lead in a minor suit, but which one? East's lowest diamond, the seven, would surely induce a diamond lead, so that was out. Whether he liked it or not, East discarded the ♣ 3, knowing full well that most partners would never read it as calling for a club lead. A gimlet-eyed partner might note that the ♣ 2 was missing and so lead a club.

In every case the ♣ 3 was discarded and West, misreading the intent of this card, led a diamond or a heart. Without a club lead to trick three, declarer was able to fulfiill his contract by pitching two club losers on the ♡ K and on dummy's fourth diamond.

Against defenders using the Lavinthal Discard SPS, declarer never had a chance. On the second spade lead, East discarded his lowest heart, the deuce. This demanded a lead in the lower ranking of the other two plain suits, a club. In compliance with his partner's discard SPS, West led a club, letting his partner take two club tricks to set the contract.

4. UNUSUAL SUIT-PREFERENCE SIGNALS

Whenever a defender purposely makes an unusual lead or play recognizable as contrary to accepted use, the inference is suit-preference. Unwittingly you might term such a play as a false-card. However, its purpose differs because the defender has no intent to deceive. His aim is to relay vital information to his partner.

Suit-preference signals may be made in many forms, each simple and logical. Unbeknown to many players, even to some who profess a great knowledge of bridge, irregular leads and plays have entered a new realm, that of bringing to partner's attention vital information which is used to gain extra tricks. I have found it logical to endow unusual defensive leads and plays with the implication of suit-preference.

Suppose that your partner pre-empts three in a suit or overcalls at two or three. Your immediate reaction is that your partner has at least six cards in his bid suit. Suppose that partner opens the deuce of his bid suit. This unusual lead of his probable sixth-best alerts you and you muse, "What is my partner trying to get across to me?"

Suddenly you realize that he must have a potent reason for his unusual and irregular lead, — surely not his fourth-best. What else could it be but suit-preference? Your partner is calling for a lead in a lower-ranking suit. Conversely if he opens the nine, he wants a higher-ranking suit led.

Suppose that your partner opened 3 ♣ and he is void in diamonds. The opposing side bought the hand for 4 ♠. Seeing no chance of promoting his club suit, your partner led the ♣ 2. This was good thinking by him and his intent was recognized by you as well as by declarer. If you hold the right cards, this message may let you do a lot of damage to declarer.

Average as well as some top-flight players, not knowing better, often pass up the opportunity of giving their partners a suit-preference signal when holding a suit headed by three or more touching honors. Perhaps these players do not realize how simple it is.

Suppose that you are on lead against 3 NT and you hold ♣ K–Q–J–x–x–x plus the ♠ A for your entry. Also your partner might be reluctant to lead a spade because declarer had bid spades. Obviously declarer is counting on bringing home 3 NT with dummy's great diamond suit. How can you indicate to your partner that your entry is in spades? The answer lies in how suit-preference is indicated by your handling of your honor sequence when your three honors are EQUALS.

The normal lead from K-Q-J is the king. What risk do you incur if you first lead the queen or the jack? Rarely will declarer at notrump take his ace on the initial lead. When he holds up on the first trick, you now have the chance to flash a signal to your partner. ALWAYS ON THE SECOND LEAD, LEAD WHAT WOULD HAVE BEEN YOUR NORMAL CARD IN THE FIRST PLACE. Thus to direct a spade lead, you would open your ♣ Q. Next your king appears and your partner knows (also declarer) that your irregular leads imply suit-preference. Partner will know that you hold at least three touching honors including the jack. You elected to make the unusual lead of the queen, which is higher than the jack. This indicates your entry in a higher-ranking suit. By the same token, should your entry be in a lower-ranking suit, you would open with the jack, which would be recognized as irregular when next your king appears. Your partner will know that you hold the queen, and because you elected to lead first the jack, which is lower-ranking, you are directing a lead in a lower-ranking suit.

Holding ♣ K–Q–J–x–x–x plus the ♡ A you defend against 3 NT and your partner opens a club. Again dummy has a great diamond suit that declarer expects to set up and run. Normally you would follow suit with your ♣ J, but you want to show suit-preference. With diamonds excluded, the two remaining suits are spades and hearts. Because your entry is in the lower-ranking heart suit, you first make the irregular follow-suit play of the queen. Remember that you have at your disposal either the king or queen with which to make an irregular play. When declarer reluctantly holds up his ace, your next lead clears the atmosphere. Always on the second lead or play the normal honor appears. In this case it is the jack. Again your partner knows that you also hold the king, — because you never make an irregular lead or play of these honors (K-Q-J) with less than three touching honors. Because you elected to make first the irregular queen play rather than the irregular king play, your partner knows that you want the lower-ranking suit led, in this case a heart.

In the deals that follow you will find ample proof how unusual suit-preference signals give the defenders much more vital information.

♠ ♡ ◇ ♣ ◇ ♡ ♠ ♡ ◇ ♣ ◇ ♡ ♠

Old bridge players never die;

They simply go down with honors.

George S. Coffin

♠ ♡ ◇ ♣ ◇ ♡ ♠ ♡ ◇ ♣ ◇ ♡ ♠

Double dummy defense was achieved on the next deal via suit-preference signals. The non-forcing two-bid shows a hand below standards to open one yet a fair to good six-card suit as the mainstay. This 2 ♠ bid plus sound inferences led the way to a killing line of defense.

Deal 34 Coffin Nails

North:
♠ Q 9 6 2
♡ 8 7 6 5 2
◇ A Q 5
♣ Q

West:
♠ A K J 8 7 3
♡ 10 9 3
◇ —
♣ 8 7 6 2

East:
♠ 10
♡ A Q J 4
◇ K 9 8 7 6 2
♣ 4 3

South:
♠ 5 4
♡ K
◇ J 10 4 3
♣ A K J 10 9 5

West	North	East	South
2 ♠	Pass	Pass	3 ♣
Pass	Pass	Pass	

West led the ♠ K and saw his partner drop the ten, clearly a singleton, for an echo with a doubleton would be lunatic in the face of dummy's spades.

Next West led the ♠ 3, clearly his lowest spade with the deuce visible in dummy. This sixth best from an advertised six-card suit East read as an UNUSUAL SPS, directing the lead of the lower ranking of the other two plain suits, a diamond. Rightly East read West as void of diamonds.

So East returned a diamond that West ruffed. East led the ◇ 2 as a SPS, directing the lead of the lower ranking of the other two plain suits, a heart. West read this so, for if the ◇ 2 were a usual fourth best, declarer would hold six diamonds and he would have bid them.* So West returned a heart to East's ace, and West ruffed another diamond for the fifth defensive trick.

Next declarer ruffed West's second heart lead and drew trumps, but he was set another trick. East drove this last nail into the coffin when he finally scored his ◇ K, which he knew all the time was safe.

---

*If South holds less than six diamonds, the ◇ 2 cannot possibly be a fourth-best lead. Editor.

In the next deal a defender made a suit-preference signal based on an irregular honor-card play, which was clearly recognizable. This represents a gain in communications heretofore thought impossible by any honest signals.

Deal 35 An Unusual Ace

	North	
	♠ 8 7	
	♡ 9 6	
	♢ K J 10 8	
	♣ K J 10 4 3	
West		**East**
♠ J 9 6 4		♠ A K Q 10 5 3 2
♡ A		♡ 3 2
♢ 9 6 5 4 2		♢ A Q
♣ 9 7 2		♣ 6 5
	South	
	♠ —	
	♡ K Q J 10 8 7 5 4	
	♢ 7 3	
	♣ A Q 8	

West	North	East	South
——	——	1 ♠	4 ♡
4 ♠	Pass	Pass	5 ♡
Double	Pass	Pass	Pass

East and West can bid and make 5 ♠ against any defense. In the crowded auction, West took the only logical action, doubling 5 ♡.

West opened the ♠ 4, and East realized that declarer would ruff. It was impossible for declarer to hold even a single spade in view of West's raise to 4 ♠. So East played the ♠ A! When West saw declarer ruff it, he recognized the unusual ace as a suit-preference signal. Knowing that the queen was East's normal play, West read the ace play as directing the lead of the higher ranking of the other two plain suits, a diamond. If instead East wanted a club lead, he would have played the ♠ K to the first trick.

Next declarer lost a trump honor to West's ace. West, alerted by his partner's SPS, returned a diamond. East won two diamond tricks, setting declarer one trick.

The SPS saved West from making a guess after winning the ♡ A. If West had guessed wrong by leading a club, declarer would have made 5 ♡ doubled with an extra trick to boot.

After the hand was played, declarer turned to West and said, "You were lucky to guess the diamond return." West smiled as he asked declarer, "Did you miss the suit-preference implication of my partner's ♠ A play?" Declarer answered, "I thought that the ♠ A was normal with you leading away from the king." "Quite so," replied West, "but I had jack fourth. It was easy for me to read my partner's suit-preference signal."

Situations occur where a deviation from normal play is proper for tactical reasons. In the next deal an irregular lead is made with a purpose, — to coax a suit-preference signal from partner. Only this lead could break the contract, barring a double dummy spade opening.

Deal 36 Premature Transfer

North:
♠ K 7 2
♡ 9
♢ K 10 8 7 4 3
♣ A 8 6

West:
♠ Q 10 8
♡ K 10 7 5 3
♢ 9 6 2
♣ K 5

East:
♠ A J 9 5
♡ A Q J 8 4 2
♢ J 5
♣ 2

South:
♠ 6 4 3
♡ 6
♢ A Q
♣ Q J 10 9 7 4 3

West	North	East	South
——	——	1 ♡	3 ♣
3 ♡	Pass	4 ♡	Pass
Pass	5 ♣	Pass	Pass
Double	Pass	Pass	Pass

A wooden West would open the ♡ 5 to East's ace. This premature transfer of the lead to East would collapse the defense. The defenders would have no way to get three spade tricks which are there for the taking if West is on lead to trick two. And if East fails to cash his ♠ A, declarer will fulfill his contract, — plus an extra trick.

West was not a parrot. He knew that rules can be broken if one has a gainful reason, so he opened the ♡ K. It was obvious, even before the opening lead, to both defenders that hearts could go unruffed no more than once. West avoided the normal fourth-best heart lead because he sensed that it may be important to retain the lead.

The ♡ K lead coaxed East to play the ♡ Q as a SPS. Recognizing this unnecessarily high card as a command to lead the higher ranking of the other two plain suits, West shifted to a spade, leading the queen. The ♠ K was trapped and the defense ran three spade tricks. It so happened that West won the third spade trick and he quickly led the ♣ 5, hoping to dupe declarer. Declarer, who knew that he was down and out, refused to take the count. He let the ♣ 5 ride to his hand, and he took the balance. He went down two doubled because West did not play like a parrot.

Never give up because your hand looks worthless. By paying attention to messages transmitted by your partner's cards, you may find that declarer's defeat can result from your thoughtful action. In the next deal an alert partnership found the key which defeated an apparently ironclad contract.

Deal 37 Chance To Be A Hero

♠ 9 7
♡ K J 7 4 3
◇ K J 10
♣ K J 9

♠ J
♡ 8 6
◇ 8 7 5 2
♣ 10 8 7 6 4 2

♠ A K Q 10 5 3
♡ 5
◇ A Q 6 3
♣ 5 3

♠ 8 6 4 2
♡ A Q 10 9 2
◇ 9 4
♣ A Q

South	West	North	East
1 ♡	Pass	3 ♡	3 ♠
Pass	Pass	4 ♡	Pass
Pass	Pass		

You may not like East's chicken-hearted pass over 4 ♡. You would bid 4 ♠ and go down one.

This time aggressive bidding fails because laying low proved to be the better policy.

West opened the ♠ J which East overtook with

the ACE. You may ask, "Isn't the queen normally the right play?" Yes, but the unusual ace play is proper here to furnish a gainful inference.

To trick two East led the ♠ Q and West paused to consider East's unusual choice of honors from ♠ A-K-Q. The only inference was suit preference. Knowing that East had a choice of an unusual ace or king play, — because the ace ranked higher, it directed the lead of the higher ranking of the other two plain suits, a diamond. West concluded that now was his chance to be a hero. Obviously East urgently needed a lead through dummy's diamonds. West trumped his partner's good trick and returned a diamond. So East took two diamond tricks and defeated declarer.*

Without playing SPS's, East wins the ♠ J with the queen and leads the ♠ 10. If West ruffs, he would probably make the wrong choice and return a club, dummy's weaker suit.

If East held ♣ A-Q instead of ◇ A-Q, how would he direct a club lead? East would overtake the ♠ J with the king, then lead the ♠ Q. This definitely shows suit preference for the lower ranking of the other two plain suits, the club suit.

---

*Cook: On the ♠ J opening, East can play the ♠ 10 as a SPS, asking for a diamond shift which West, still on lead, should make. Even if West holds another spade, he should shift. This defense is equally effective as the above, but not as artistic. **Editor.**

Freak hands occur more often than mathematical frequency percentages indicate. The cause may be an an imperfect shuffle, or starting play with a new pack, or the way cards cling together when piled in tricks. Each bridge session has its share of what I like to call crackpot hands. In the next deal a chain of suit-preference signals proved useful.

Deal 38 Chain Gang

North:
♠ A K Q 10 7 3
♡ K 6 4
◇ 8 7
♣ 8 2

West:
♠ 9 6 5 4
♡ 5 2
◇ —
♣ Q J 10 9 6 4 3

East:
♠ 8 2
♡ J 3
◇ K J 10 9 6 5 4 2
♣ A

South:
♠ J
♡ A Q 10 9 8 7
◇ A Q 3
♣ K 7 5

West	North	East	South
3 ♣	3 ♠	4 ◇	4 ♡
Pass	Pass	Pass	

If you do not see the East-West hands, a 6 ♡ contract looks reasonable, yet unsound in this crowded auction that suggests freak shapes and ruffing dangers. Also, North could have more spades without the ♠ A.

West fingered his ♣ Q but before leading, he wondered how to cash in on his diamond void. He knew that partnership co-operation is vital. It might be well to apprise his partner to lead a diamond. So West abandoned the ♣ Q and instead led the THREE of clubs. This was an SPS that was readily recognizable. If East could win the ♣ 3, he knew that West wanted a lead in the lower ranking of the other two plain suits, a diamond. Luckily East won with the ♣ A and returned a diamond. East joined the chain-gang procession of unusual SPS's by leading the TWO of diamonds. Declarer finessed his ◇ Q and West ruffed. West repeated his unusual SPS by returning his bottom club to show another trump in hand for another possible diamond ruff. East ruffed the club and returned a diamond honor, declarer played his ace, and West broke the camel's back when he ruffed to score a one-trick set.

This deal shows how a chain of three suit-preference signals in one hand is possible.

The tactical reluctance of declarer to take an ace at once can be the means to let one defender transmit vital information to his partner. The next deal illustrates this principle, — useful at notrump.

Deal 39 Strange Pictures

West	North	East
	♠ Q 7 4 ♡ K 8 ♢ A J 10 9 7 4 ♣ 10 9	
♠ 9 8 ♡ A 6 3 2 ♢ 8 ♣ K Q J 4 3 2		♠ 10 6 5 3 2 ♡ 9 7 5 4 ♢ K 6 ♣ 6 5
	♠ A K J ♡ Q J 10 ♢ Q 5 3 2 ♣ A 8 7	

West	North	East	South
——	Pass	Pass	1 NT
2 ♣	3 ♢	Pass	3 NT
Pass	Pass	Pass	

West knew that the regular lead from K-Q-J is the king. Despite this he opened the ♣ J. The safety of this unusual lead is based on declarer's reluctance to take the ace on the opening lead, which gives West the chance NEXT to make his normal first-trick lead. This at once corrects any false impression that his partner might get. Of course East was mystified momentarily, but the fog lifted when next West led the ♣ K, taken by declarer's ace. It was clear to all that West had K-Q-J.

When the ♣ K appeared, the strange picture took form. Because West led the ♣ J, the lower ranking from a choice of queen and jack, the ♣ J lead could only be read as directing the lead of the lower ranking of two suits. The auction eliminated diamonds from suit-preference consideration. East knew that West wanted a heart returned, not a spade.

Declarer had to have the diamond finesse win, but it lost to East's king. East, no longer on guess, returned a heart to his partner's ace. West cashed four clubs, setting declarer three tricks.

Without the use of a SPS, East on lead via the ◇ K could guess wrong and return a spade.

You may ask, "Why not first open the ♣ K then lead ♣ Q to show the higher-ranking suit or ♣ J to show the lower-ranking?" The answer is simple. An UNUSUAL opening lead POSITIVELY implies suit preference. A normal opening lead suggest no particular preference.

Often a hand occurs where both defenders share glory in defeating declarer with seemingly double-dummy play. The deal below shows how an extra advantage can be gained by fooling partner.

Deal 40 A White Lie

	North	
	♠ Q 5 4 ♡ J 10 ♢ J 7 3 ♣ A 6 5 4 2	
♠ 9 8 7 3 2 ♡ 6 5 ♢ Q 10 8 6 5 2 ♣ —		♠ A 10 ♡ 8 7 2 ♢ A K 9 ♣ Q J 8 7 3
	♠ K J 6 ♡ A K Q 9 4 3 ♢ 4 ♣ K 10 9	

South	West	North	East
——	——	——	1 NT*
Double	3 ♢	Pass	Pass
3 ♡	Pass	4 ♡ (final bid)	

West opened the ♢ 2, and without batting an eyelash East popped out the ♢ A! Why did East deceive his partner by not playing the ♢ K? The reason is

*Weak notrump based on 12 to 14 high-card points.

clear if the bidding is reviewed. West, against a double, would not jump bid 3 ♢ on less than six diamonds. So South cannot have more than one diamond. By making West think that the ♢ K lay South, East showed that a second diamond lead cannot interest the defenders.

Because East and West were using suit-preference signals, East understood the message of that irregular ♢ 2 lead, NOT a fourth best. East read this lead as a suit-preference signal, calling for the lead of the lower ranking of the other two plain suits, a club.

East led the JACK of clubs, hoping that West would read it as calling for a spade lead. West ruffed, and figuring as East hoped, picked the ♠ 2. East won the ♠ A. Next East returned another club, knowing that West's ♠ 2 lead suggested that West could ruff another club, which he did and set declarer one trick.

At the other tables in a duplicate game, with similar bidding, East won the ♢ 6 lead with the king. Using primary signals exclusively, East had no way of reading his partner for a club void. East led the ♠ A then ♠ 10 in a mad quest to find the ♠ K in West and to get a spade ruff* This hope vanished, so South won ten tricks for his contract.

---

*Mad quest is right, for West gave the ♠ 2 on the ♠ A lead. East in most cases tried a club that West ruffed, but declarer still got his ten tricks. **Editor.**

On many deals the winning defense can be found if a suit-preference signal is supplemented with imagination. The next deal illustrates a play never before shown in a book.

Deal 41 First On Record

North:
♠ J 7 4 3
♡ K 4
◇ K 7 3
♣ K Q J 9

West:
♠ A 6 2
♡ 10 8
◇ 10 9 8 5 4 2
♣ 5 2

East:
♠ 8
♡ A Q 9 7 6 5 3
◇ Q 6
♣ A 8 7

South:
♠ K Q 10 9 5
♡ J 2
◇ A J
♣ 10 6 4 3

South	West	North	East
Pass	Pass	1 NT*	3 ♡
3 ♠	Pass	Pass	Pass

In a duplicate game most North-South pairs bought the hand for 3 ♠ or 4 ♠. The 3 ♠ contract was defeated by only one defending pair.

West opened the ♡ 10, going to king and ace.

*The weak notrump on 12 to 14 points.

East cleaned out all outstanding hearts with the queen, and thought, "What should I lead now?"

Figuring that his ♣ A was safe, East led another heart, hoping to promote something in his partner's hand. For this, East led his LOWEST heart. Declarer discarded the ◇ J, hoping to induce a diamond lead lest a club be ruffed. Declarer ruffed in dummy.

Meanwhile West took a reading. East's bottom-heart lead was a SPS, directing the lead of the lower ranking of the other two plain suits, a club. Presumably the SPS showed the ♣ A.

"Aha," thought West. "I'll ditch the ♣ 5 and maybe I'll get a club ruff if East has the ♣ A." Declarer led a trump from dummy to his king. The ace won. So West returned his last club, the deuce to complete his club echo, to East's ace; and West ruffed the club return for the setting trick.*

Despite defeat, declarer congratulated both opponents for their brilliant defense, **a type that is here** the first on record.

At other tables were defenders did not play SPS's, West took the bait. Declarer's ◇ J discard suggested diamond weakness, so West switched to a diamond that let declarer score nine tricks.

---

*Cook: To trick three East can instead lead a low club and later give West his club ruff. But the third heart lead also caters to promoting a trump trick if West holds ♠ Q-x. **Editor.**

Few players realize how far suit-preference signals have been developed to broadcast information instantly and effectively. In the next deal from a world championship, declarer could have been defeated. So the deal got top publicity in bridge magazines all over the world. No reflection is cast upon any player involved. However, please understand that it is not so much a matter of using SPS's as it is to have a complete partnership agreement on how to apply them.

Deal 42 Clarion Call For Trump

West	North	East
	♠ K Q 7	
	♡ J 8 5 4	
	◇ A 3 2	
	♣ K Q 8	
♠ A 10 8 6 5 2		♠ J 4 3
♡ 7 3 2		♡ A 9
◇ 8 4		◇ K Q J 10 5
♣ J 7		♣ 9 5 3
	♠ 9	
	♡ K Q 10 6	
	◇ 9 7 6	
	♣ A 10 6 4 2	

West	North	East	South
——	1 ♣	1 ◇	1 ♡
1 ♠	2 ♡	2 ♠	3 ♣
Pass	4 ♡	(final bid)	

In one room the British North-South pair bid and made 3 ♣ whereas in the other room the Americans bid and made 4 ♡. Yet 4 ♡ could have been defeated at double dummy or by defenders in complete agreement on how to apply SPS's.

West led the ◇ 8, dummy ducked and East won with his ten. East returned the ◇ K to dummy's ace. Declarer lost the ♠ K to West's ace. West, hoping to find the ♣ A in East, led a club that dummy won. Declarer parked his diamond loser on the ♠ Q and fulfilled his contract.

At the time this deal was reported, bridge writers made a big fuss about suit preference. They made much of East's wide choice of SPS's. Beyond this point they simply conjectured how suit preference could have specified a trump lead.

While normally the SPS is not used to indicate a trump lead, on this deal it would be simple. Since East held a four-card honor sequence, ◇ K-Q-J-10, we have an ideal situation where a SPS can be given to identify which one of the three remaining suits should be led.

East could see that declarer's holdup of the ◇ A on trick one was an effort to avoid losing two diamond tricks. To break the contract, two diamond tricks were needed, plus West's ♠ A (placed by the bidding) and East's ♡ A.

To counter declarer's purpose, East should on trick one play the QUEEN of diamonds, then lead the TEN of diamonds losing to ace. At this point West would recognize that East held ◇ K-Q-J-10; for if declarer held the ◇ K, he would have won the first trick. West, knowing that partner's normal play to trick one was the ◇ 10, should recognize that the ◇ Q play was an unusual SPS, identifying which one of the three other suits should be led. East should reason that his partner could have played the king, the queen or the jack on trick one. SINCE EAST SELECTED THE QUEEN, HE SPECIFIED THE MIDDLE-RANKING OF THE OTHER THREE SUITS, HEARTS.

Had East desired a spade lead, he would have played the ◇ K on trick one; or had East wanted a club, he would have played the ◇ J.

When making this type of play, the second-trick lead MUST BE THE HONOR CARD THAT WOULD BE NORMALLY PLAYED ON THE FIRST TRICK. When the second honor is led, partner will know that the unusual play of the two honors imply suit preference.

To trick three declarer would lead a spade honor from dummy and East should play the JACK, a repeat SPS, to make doubly sure that West would lead a heart when he gets on lead. Then West, knowing that East's

♠ J play was not forced, should be shot at sunrise if he failed to lead a heart.

West wins the ♠ A, leads a heart to East's ace, and East cashes the second diamond trick to set the contract.

Freedom of action is preserved at all times if East, having the chance to give a SPS, rejects the opportunity to give this signal.

If East's 1 ♢ bid was bolstered by the ♡ K instead of the ♡ A, East would have no preference and he would play his diamond honors normally, first the ten then the king. West would then know that he is on his own and free to rely on judgement. Negative inferences can sometimes be as important as positive ones.

♠ ♡ ♢ ♣ ♢ ♡ ♠ ♡ ♢ ♣ ♢ ♡ ♠

"In all the bridge-game places

The rats get at the aces."

QUIZZES

Here we offer you more than 40 quiz deals on all types of defensive play. Of these a realistically small proportion illustrates suit-preference signals, scattered at random throughout to keep you on your toes.

Solutions to the quizzes appear in the back of the book.

Deal 43 Quiz North-South Vulnerable

North
♣ K

East, Dummy
♠ Q J 8 6
♡ Q 8 3
◇ Q 6 4
♣ 8 7 6

South, You
♠ 7 4 2
♡ A K J
◇ 10 8 7 3
♣ A 3 2

West	North	East	South
1 ♠	2 ♣	Pass	3 ♣
3 ◇	Pass	3 ♠ (final bid)	

North leads the ♣ K. How do you, playing South, signal so as to get your partner to lead a heart?

Deal 44 Quiz No Score

North
♢ A Q 7

West, Dummy
♠ K J 10 7
♡ Q J 3
♢ 9 6 4
♣ A Q 2

East
♢ J 10 8

South, You
♠ 8 6 3 2
♡ 10 8 5
♢ 2
♣ J 10 9 7 4

West	North	East	South
—	—	1 ♡	Pass
1 ♠	3 ♢	Pass	Pass
3 ♡	Pass	Pass	Pass

South opened the ♢ 2 that North won with his ace. North cashed the ♢ Q and South discarded the ♠ 3. North led the ♢ 7 which South ruffed.

What should you, playing South, lead to trick four? Why?

Deal 45 Quiz No Score

North
♡ 10 K 3

West, Dummy
♠ 8 7 4
♡ J 7 4
◇ A J 10 9 5
♣ 7 4

East
♡ 5 9 A
◇ 7

South, You
♠ Q 9 6
♡ Q 8 6 2
◇ K 8 2
♣ 9 6 2

West	North	East	South
Pass	Pass	1 ♣	Pass
1 ◇	Pass	2 NT	Pass
3 NT	Pass	Pass	Pass

Sitting South you lead the ♡ 2 which North's ten wins. Next North wins the ♡ K then loses the ♡ 3 to East's ♡ A. On this third heart lead do you play the ♡ 8 or the ♡ Q?

To trick four East led the ◇ 7. Which diamond do you play?

Deal 46 Quiz No Score

North
♣ 8 5 9
♡ 3

West, Dummy
♠ K Q
♡ Q 10 8
◇ K Q 6 5 3
♣ 7 3 2

East

♡ 5 7

♣ 6 4

South, You
♠ 9 8 4
♡ A 6 4 2
◇ 8 4
♣ K Q J 10

South	West	North	East
—	—	Pass	1 ♡
Pass	2 ◇	Pass	3 ◇
Pass	4 ♡ (final bid)		

Sitting South, you lead the ♣ K, then ♣ Q, which both win, then the ♣ J that East ruffs. East leads the ♡ 7.

Do you play your ♡ A immediately? Or later?

If later and East continues trumps, which trump lead do you win.

After you make the ♡ A, what do you lead?

Deal 47 Quiz North-South Vulnerable

North
♠ 3
◇ 4

West, Dummy
♠ Q 9 8 5 2
♡ 8 4 3
◇ A 9
♣ A K J

East
♠ A
◇ 3

South, You
♠ K J 10
♡ Q 7
◇ Q J 8 7 5 2
♣ 5 3

West	North	East	South
—	Pass	1 ♡	Pass
1 ♠	Pass	1 NT	Pass
3 NT	Pass	Pass	Pass

You are South and you lead the ◇ 7, which dummy wins with the ◇ A. The ♠ 2 then goes to declarer's ♠ A. How do you plan to defend?

Deal 48 Quiz East-West Vulnerable

North
♠ 5 8 9
♡ K 10

West
♡ 4 A
◇ A K 4

East, Dummy
♠ A K J 7
♡ 9 8 7
◇ 8 7 5 3
♣ A J

South, You
♠ Q 4 3 2
♡ 2
◇ J 10 9 2
♣ K 5 3 2

West	North	East	South
1 ◇	3 ♡	3 ♠	Pass
3 NT	Pass	Pass	Pass

North led the ♡ K, which won, then the ♡ 10, which West won with his ♡ A. West played the ◇ A, ◇ K, then ◇ 4, on which North discarded three spades and you are on lead. To trick six, which card do you lead? Why?

Deal 49 Quiz

North
♠ 4 9
♡ 2 6

West, Dummy
♠ Q 7 3
♡ K Q 8 3
◇ 10 9 3
♣ 6 5 3

East
♠ 2 J
♡ 9 A

South, You
♠ A K 10 6
♡ 5 4
◇ A J 5
♣ J 9 8 4

West	North	East	South
—	—	1 ♡	Double
2 ♡	Pass	3 ♡ (final bid)	

You, playing South, led the ♠ K and North dropped the ♠ 4. Next you led the ♡ 5 to declarer's nine. Why did you lead the ♡ 5 instead of the ♡ 4?

Next declarer won the ♡ A, then led the ♠ J, which you grabbed with your ♠ A, and North dropped the ♠ 9. What does North's card mean?

What do you lead to trick four? Why?

Deal 50 Quiz North-South Vulnerable

North
♡ 5 A 6
◇ Q J 10

West
♠ 4 8 9 J
♡ Q J

East, Dummy
♠ 7 2
♡ 10 8 2
◇ 8 6 3 2
♣ 9 5 4 2

South, You
♠ Q 5 3
♡ K 4 3
◇ A K 5 4
♣ K J 3

West	North	East	South
2 ♠	Pass	2 NT	Pass
4 ♠	Pass	Pass	Pass

Your partner, North, leads the ◇ Q, which West ruffs. West returns the ♡ Q, which your ♡ K wins. West ruffs your ◇ K, and North wins the ♡ J return with his ace. West ruffs a third diamond lead, and he leads the ♠ J, on which North discards the ♡ 6.

How do you play?

Deal 51 Quiz No Score

North
♢ 4

East, Dummy
♠ A J 7
♡ A 10
♢ 7 2
♣ A Q J 10 8 4

South, You
♠ 10 6 4 2
♡ J 7 6 3
♢ A Q 6
♣ K 5

South	West	North	East
Pass	Pass	Pass	1 ♣
Pass	1 ♡	Pass	3 ♣
Pass	3 NT (final bid)		

North opens the ♢ 4 and dummy plays low. Sitting South, which diamond do you play?

Why?

Deal 52 Quiz No Score

North
◇ K

East, Dummy
♠ A Q 9
♡ J 7 5 2
◇ J 10 9 2
♣ 9 7

South, You
♠ K J 6 3
♡ Q 10 9
◇ 8 3
♣ J 10 8 4

South	West	North	East
Pass	1 ♡	Pass	2 ♡
Pass	4 ♡ (final bid)		

North opens the ◇ K. Sitting South, which diamond do you play on the king? Why?

Deal 53 Quiz East-West Vulnerable

South, You
♠ K
♡ A K 7 4
◇ A K Q 6
♣ Q J 9 6

West	North	East	South
Pass	Pass	1 ♠	Double
Pass	Pass!	Pass	

What card should you lead?

Deal 54 Quiz No Score

North
♢ 4
♠ 4
♣ J

West, Dummy
♠ 9 8 3
♡ J 5 4 2
♢ A K
♣ K Q 7 6

East
♢ 6
♠ K
♣ 4

South, You
♠ J 7
♡ K 8 7 6 3
♢ 5 3
♣ A 8 5 2

West	North	East	South
—	—	1 ♢	Pass
2 NT	Pass	3 ♢	Pass
4 ♢	Pass	6 ♢ (final bid)	

Playing South you led the ♢ 5 to ♢ K in dummy. Dummy led the ♠ 3, North played ♠ 4, and ♠ K won in East. East led ♣ 4, which you won with ♣ A, and North, your partner, followed suit with the ♣ J.

To trick four, what do you lead?

Deal 55 Quiz No Score

North
♠ K

East, Dummy
♠ J 5
♡ K 10
♢ A 9 8 5 2
♣ K J 8 5

South, You
♠ A Q 10 6 3
♡ A 8
♢ J 7 3
♣ 10 7 3

South	West	North	East
1 ♠	2 ♡	2 ♠	3 ♢
Pass	3 ♡	Pass	4 ♡
Pass	Pass	Pass	

Your partner opens the ♠ K. Although playing suit-preference signals, he always opens the best card of his partner's bid suit.

What card do you play to trick one? Trick two?

Deal 56 Quiz No Score

North
♣ 4

East, Dummy
♠ A K
♡ Q 10 9 4
◇ Q 10 3
♣ J 9 6 3

South, You
♠ Q 10 8 7 4
♡ 6 3 2
◇ 7 6
♣ A 5 2

West	North	East	South
1 ♡	Pass	3 ♡	Pass
4 ♡	Pass	Pass	Pass

North opens the ♣ 4. How should you, playing South, plan the defense?

♠ ♡ ◇ ♣ ◇ ♡ ♠ ♡ ◇ ♣ ◇ ♡ ♠

"and in those days
the game was
played wistfully."

Deal 57 Quiz No Score

North
♡ A K 10
♣ 5 4

West, Dummy
♠ Q 10 6
♡ 9 6
◇ K 5 3
♣ A 9 8 6 3

East
♡ 4 5 Q
♣ 7 J

South, You
♠ 9 8 5 3 2
♡ J
◇ 10 8 7 6
♣ Q 10 2

South	West	North	East
—	—	1 ♡	1 NT
Pass	3 NT (final bid)		

You, South, lead the ♡ J which your partner wins with the ♡ A. Next he lays down the ♡ K, then leads ♡ 10 to East's queen, on which dummy discards the ♠ 6. This spade discard indicates that declarer is showing no fear in the spade suit.

To trick four declarer leads the ♣ 7, going to your ten and dummy's ace, and your partner plays the ♣ 5. On dummy's low club return your partner plays the ♣ 4, and the ♣ J loses to your queen.

What do you lead to trick six? Why?

Deal 58 Quiz No Score

North
♣ 5 A 2

West, Dummy
♠ A Q J
♡ Q J 10
◇ K J 5 3
♣ K 6 3

East
♠ 3

♣ 4 7

South, You
♠ 10 7 4 2
♡ 7
◇ A 8 6
♣ Q J 10 9 8

West	North	East	South
—	Pass	1 ♠	Pass
3 NT*	Pass	4 ♡	Pass
4 ♠	Pass	Pass	Pass

As South you open the ♣ Q, which wins. Next you lead the ♣ J, going to king and your partner's ace. North returns the third club, which East ruffs. East leads the ◇ 10. What do you play? Why?

---

*Or 2 ◇ forcing, then over 2 ♡ West jumps to 4 ♠. The occasion, as here, for the direct 3 NT jump is rare. So to give the bid more practical use, Monroe Ingerberman and George Sorter of Chicago invented the Sorter Convention. In this a direct jump to 3 NT over partner's 1 ♡ or 1 ♠ opening is an

(Continued on page 124)

Deal 59 Quiz North-South Vulnerable

North
◇ 7

West
◇ 8

East, Dummy
♠ A Q 7
♡ Q 8 3
◇ Q J 10 4 3
♣ K 9

South, You
♠ 8
♡ A 10 7 6 2
◇ A 9 5 2
♣ Q 7 5

South	West	North	East
Pass	1 ♠	Pass	2 ◇
Pass	2 ♠	Pass	4 ♠
Pass	Pass	Pass	

Your partner, North, leads the ◇ 7, which you win with your ◇ A.

What card do you lead to trick two? Why?

---

artificial force to guarantee game support in opener's major. The purpose is to use the DIRECT jump to three in opener's major as a non-forcing LIMIT bid on 10 to 12 support points. Both the Jacoby-Smith and Kaplan-Sheinwold schools have adopted all this. **Editor.**

Deal 60 Quiz Game All

North
♡ 5
◇ 3

West
♡ A
♣ 4

East, Dummy
♠ K Q 7
♡ Q 9 6
◇ J 10 2
♣ A K Q 3

South, You
♠ A 5 3
♡ K J 10 8 2
◇ A 7 4
♣ 8 5

South	West	North	East
1 ♡	Pass	Pass	Double
Pass	1 NT	Pass	2 NT
Pass	3 NT (final bid)		

North, your partner, leads the ♡ 5, and your ♡ 8 forces the ace from West. He enters dummy via ♣ Q and leads the ◇ J.

How do you plan your defense to beat 3 NT?

Deal 61 Quiz North-South Vulnerable

North
♡ K

East, Dummy
♠ 10 3
♡ 9 4 2
◇ K J 8 5
♣ K 9 6 4

South, You
♠ K Q 8
♡ A J 8 5 3
◇ 7 4 3
♣ A 3

South	West	North	East
1 ♡	4 ♣	4 ♡	5 ♣
Pass	Pass	Pass	

North leads the ♡ K.

How do you plan your play to win three tricks?

Deal 62 Quiz North-South Vulnerable

North
♠ 6
♡ 2 5 6
◇ 7
♣ 2 4

West, Dummy
♠ K J 7 3
♡ 8 7 4 3
◇ K 5 4
♣ 8 5

East
♠ 2 A 5 9
♡ 10 J
◇ A

South, You
♠ 8 4
♡ A K Q 9
◇ Q J 9
♣ K J 10 3

West	North	East	South
Pass	Pass	1 ♠	Double
2 ♠	Pass	4 ♠ (final bid)	

Playing South you cash the ♡ K, then ♡ Q, and East ruffs your ♡ A. East cashes the ♠ A, dummy the ♠ K and East ruffs the heart while North discards the ♣ 2, then ♣ 4. East next lays down the ◇ A.

How do you play your diamonds? Why?

Deal 63 Quiz No Score

North
♣ 10

East, Dummy
♠ Q J 9
♡ K 10 9 8
◇ K 10 6
♣ K J 2

South, You
♠ 8 7 4 3
♡ 6 5 3 2
◇ A Q J 3
♣ A

West	North	East	South
1 NT*	Pass	3 NT** (final bid)	

North opens the ♣ 10, dummy ducks and you win with your ♣ A.

What do you lead to trick two?

---

* The weak notrump opening on 12 to 14 points.

**East gains nothing by bidding 2 ♣ Stayman to find a 4-4 heart fit, as with it the hand would probably play better at 3 NT with East's 4-3-3-3 shape.

Deal 64 Quiz No Score

North
♠ 4 7
♡ 4 6 8
◇ 3 5

West, Dummy
♠ K J 10 6
♡ A 7 5
◇ J 7
♣ K 9 7 5

East
♠ A 8 3
♡ K 8
◇ A 4

South, You
♠ 5 2
♡ J 10 2
◇ K Q 10 9 8
♣ J 4 2

West	North	East	South
1 ♣	Pass	2 ♠	Pass
3 ♠	Pass	4 ♣	Pass
4 ♠	Pass	5 ♡?	Pass
6 ♡!	Pass	6 ♠ (final bid)	

East's call of 5 ♡ is an asking bid and West's reply of 6 ♡ shows the ♡ A.

As South, you lead the ◇ K which declarer wins with ace. He pulls two rounds of trumps, plays ♡ K, ♡ A and ruffs a heart. Finally he throws you on lead with the ◇ Q. How many diamonds does East have left in his hand? How many clubs? What do you lead now?

Deal 65 Quiz No Score

North
♠ K A J
♡ A

West
♠ 3
♡ 6 10

East, Dummy
♠ 9 7 4 2
♡ 7 4
◇ A K 9
♣ A K Q 6

South, You
♠ Q
♡ 9 5 3 2
◇ Q J 10 4
♣ J 10 5 2

West	North	East	South
2 ♡*	4 ♠	5 ♡ (final bid)	

North, your partner, leads the ♠ K which wins. Next North leads the ♠ A, on which you discard the ◇ 4, and West ruffs. West leads the ♡ 10, which North's ♡ A wins. North returns the ♠ J. What do you play? Why?

---

*Weak two-bid.

Deal 66 Quiz No Score

North
♡ 10 K Q
♢ 5

West

♡ 7 5 A
♢ 7

East, Dummy
♠ K J 7
♡ 6
♢ A K J 9 4
♣ 10 8 4 2

South, You
♠ 10 9 6 2
♡ 8 4 2
♢ Q 10 8 2
♣ Q 3

South	West	North	East
—	—	1 ♡	Double
Pass	2 NT (final bid)		

This deal comes from a recent world championship in which England played against the USA.

Your partner opens ♡ 10 which wins! Next he leads ♡ K which wins, then ♡ Q to West's ace.

To trick four West finessed ♢ J to your queen.

To trick five what do you lead? Why?

Deal 67 Quiz North No Score

North
♠ 3
♡ 2

West, Dummy
♠ A
♡ 9 3
◇ A 9 4 3
♣ Q J 10 9 8 3

East
♠ 5
♡ J

South, You
♠ K J 10 9 7 2
♡ Q 10 4
◇ 6 5
♣ K 5

West	North	East	South
—	Pass	1 ♡	1 ♠
2 ♣	Pass	2 NT	Pass
3 NT	Pass	Pass	Pass

You sit South and lead the ♠ J which dummy's ♠ A won. Dummy led ♡ 3 and declarer finessed ♡ J to your queen. Clearly East holds ♠ Q-x-x for his notrump bid in the face of your 1 ♠ overcall. Odds are two to one that spades will split 2-4 in the North and East hands, so most likely East began life with ♠ Q-x-x-x. Hence a spade lead by your partner will let you get only two spade tricks. East probably holds ♡ A-K-J-x or ♡ A-K-J-x–x for his 1 ♡ bid. Why didn't East lead a club to trick two? What do you lead to trick three? Why?

Deal 68 Quiz Game All

North
♠ 2
◇ 9

West
♠ 10

◇ J

East, Dummy
♠ K J 8 4
♡ Q 9 5
◇ 6 5
♣ A J 9 2

South, You
♠ A Q 6
♡ 6 2
◇ A Q 10 8 3
♣ 10 8 5

South	West	North	East
1 ◇	Double	Pass	2 ♠
Pass	2 NT	Pass	3 ♣
Pass	3 NT (final bid)		

Your partner, North, opense the ◇ 9 which you let run to declarer's jack. Declarer lets the ♠ 10 run up to you.

How do you plan your defense?

How do you begin it?

Deal 69 Quiz North-South Vulnerable

North
♢ 2
♣ 6

West, Dummy
♠ A 5
♡ 8 3
♢ 8 6 4 3
♣ 9 5 4 3 2

East
♢ A
♣ A Q

South, You
♠ 6 4
♡ 10 9 7 6
♢ K Q J 10
♣ K 8 7

West	North	East	South
Pass	Pass	1 ♣	Pass
2 ♣	Pass	3 NT (final bid)	

You are South. You lead the ♢ K, which East wins with ♢ A. East lays down the ♣ A, then ♣ Q.

Do you take the ♣ K now?

When you take your ♣ K, which suit do you lead? Why?

Deal 70 Quiz North-South Vulnerable

North
♠ 2

West, Dummy
♠ 4
♡ Q 5
◇ Q 9 7 5
♣ K Q 10 8 7 3

East
♠ A
♡ 2

South, You
♠ Q J 10 9 8 3
♡ A 6 3
◇ K 10 4
♣ 2

West	North	East	South
Pass	Pass	1 ♡	1 ♠
2 ♣	Pass	2 NT	Pass
3 ♣	Pass	3 NT (final bid)	

You, South, lead the ♠ Q which declarer wins with ♠ A. Declarer leads the ♡ 2.

Why did he persist to 3 NT over West's signoff rebid of 3 ♣?

Why didn't East lead a club? Should you pass the heart lead?

How do you plan to score five tricks?

Deal 71 Quiz North-South Vulnerable

North
♠ K
♡ 6

West
♠ A
♡ Q

East, Dummy
♠ 9 7
♡ K 8 5
◇ 8 5 2
♣ K Q J 10 5

South, You
♠ 8 5 4 3
♡ A 7 2
◇ 9 6 3
♣ A 6 4

West	North	East	South
1 ♡	1 ♠	2 ♡	2 ♠
3 ♡	Pass	4 ♡ (final bid)	

Your partner leads the ♠ K which goes to West's ♠ A. West leads the ♡ Q.

Playing South, how do you plan the defense?

Deal 72 Quiz No Score

North
♡ 10 J 5

West, Dummy
♠ K
♡ 9 3 2
◇ 9 7 4 2
♣ A Q J 6 2

East
♡ 6 7 A

South, You
♠ A 8 6
♡ K Q 8 4
◇ J 6 3
♣ 9 8 5

West	North	East	South
Pass	Pass	1 ♠	Pass
2 ♣	Pass	2 NT	Pass
3 NT	Pass	Pass	Pass

As South, you lead the ♡ 4 and North's ♡ 10 wins. North continues with the ♡ J that also wins. But when East takes North's ♡ 5 with the ace, do you play the ♡ Q or ♡ K? Why?

Deal 73 Quiz No Score

North
♡ J

West, Dummy
♠ A 10 6 2
♡ 8
◇ K Q 5 4
♣ A J 10 2

East
♡ 2

South, You
♠ 7 3
♡ A K 10 6 3
◇ 7 6
♣ K Q 5 4

South	West	North	East
1 ♡	Double	3 ♡	3 ♠
4 ♡	4 ♠	Pass	Pass
5 ♡	5 ♠ (final bid)		

You, South, lead the ♡ K and North plays the ♡ J. What does this card mean?

What should you lead to trick two?

Deal 74 Quiz East-West Vulnerable

South, You
♠ A 6
♡ J 9 7
◇ K Q J 8 7
♣ K 7 2

West	North	East	South
Pass	Pass	1 ♣	1 ◇
1 ♠	2 ◇	5 ♣ (final bid)	

East on your right becomes declarer. What do you lead?

♠ ♡ ◇ ♣ ◇ ♡ ♠ ♡ ◇ ♣ ◇ ♡ ♠

"Oh, Yes, Miss Truesdale. My Patrick says there's two kind of bridge players, them that's good and them that peek."

♠ ♡ ◇ ♣ ◇ ♡ ♠ ♡ ◇ ♣ ◇ ♡ ♠

Deal 75 Quiz No Score

North
♢ J

East, Dummy
♠ K J 3
♡ A Q 8
♢ A 7 3
♣ 9 6 3 2

South, You
♠ A Q 10 9 6
♡ 10 4 3 2
♢ K 8 5
♣ J

South	West	North	East
Pass	1 NT*	Pass	3 NT
Pass	Pass	Pass	

North opens the ♢ J, dummy ducks, and your king wins.

What card do you lead to trick two? Why?

*The weak notrump on 12 to 14 high-card points.

Deal 76 Quiz East-West Have Game

North
♠ K 2
♢ 2

West
♠ 9

♢ J 10

East, Dummy
♠ A 10
♡ A 4 2
♢ Q 8 7 4
♣ K 6 4 2

South, You
♠ 6 5 3
♡ K Q 8 6
♢ A 3
♣ J 10 9 8

West	North	East	South
1 ♢	Pass	2 ♢!	Pass
3 ♢	Pass	5 ♢ (final bid)	

East's raise to 2 ♢ was the forcing variety, a part of the modern and popular weak notrump system. When West rebid his diamonds, he suggested a six-card suit with a minimum of high-card values to open, so East preferred the diamond game that looked safer than a notrump game. East was right, as North-South can hold any notrump contract to seven tricks.

Against 5 ♢ North led the ♠ K, won by dummy's ♠ A. South ducked a diamond, then won declarer's second diamond lead, on which North discarded the ♠ 2. What do you lead to trick four?

Deal 77 Quiz All Vulnerable

North
♠ 6
♡ A 7 4
◇ 2
♣ A

West, Dummy
♠ 10 3
♡ 10 9 3 2
◇ K Q 10 8
♣ J 8 7

East

♡ 8 6 5

♣ 10 9 6

South, You
♠ 9 8 2
♡ K Q J
◇ A 9
♣ K 5 4 3 2

West	North	East	South
—	—	1 ♠	Pass
1 NT	Pass	2 ♠ (final bid)	

Playing South, you led the ♡ K, which North overtook with the ♡ A. North cashed the ♣ A, then returned the ♡ 7 to your jack. Figuring that ♣ A surely to be dry, you returned a low club that North ruffed. He returned the heart to your queen.

Trick six you won with the ♣ K, on which North discarded the ◇ 2.

What is East's shape?

What significance, if any, do you attach to that ♢ 2 discard?

What do you lead to trick seven? Why?

Deal 78 Quiz North-South Vulnerable

North
♡ A

East, Dummy
♠ A K Q
♡ K 5 4
♢ —
♣ 10 9 7 6 5 4 2

South, You
♠ J 6 2
♡ Q 10 8 3
♢ A 8 5 4
♣ 8 3

West	North	East	South
—	1 ♡	2 ♣	2 ♡
2 ♠	Pass	3 ♠	Pass
4 ♠	Pass	Pass	Pass

You are playing in a match-point pairs duplicate game. Your partner, North, and you have agreed not to open four-card majors.

North led the ♡ A and dummy played low.

How many hearts does West hold?

Which heart do you play on partner's ace? Why?

Deal 79 Quiz No Score

North
♠ K

East, Dummy
♠ 6 4 3
♡ K J 7 2
◇ J 4
♣ A Q 10 7

South, You
♠ A J 10 8 5
♡ A 9
◇ K 10 7 3
♣ 8 5

South	West	North	East
1 ♠	3 ♡	4 ♠	5 ♡
Double	Pass	Pass	Pass

North leads the ♠ K. Which spade do you play?

Deal 80 Quiz No Score

North
♡ K Q

West
♡ 3 4

East, Dummy
♠ K Q 10 5
♡ J 5
◇ A Q 10 9 2
♣ 10 5

South, You
♠ 9 7 4 3 2
♡ 9 7 2
◇ 7 5
♣ K 6 2

West	North	East	South
1 ♣	1 ♡	1 ♠	Pass
3 ♣	Pass	3 ◇	Pass
4 ♣	Pass	5 ♣ (final bid)	

North leads the ♡ K that wins.
Next North leads the ♡ Q that also wins.
How do you follow suit on these two tricks? Why?

Deal 81 Quiz East-West Vulnerable

North
♣ Q

East, Dummy
♠ Q 10 8 3
♡ Q J 9 3
◇ A Q 8 5
♣ 2

South, You
♠ 9 7 5
♡ A K
◇ K 6 2
♣ A 9 8 6 4

West dealt and bid 1 ♠; East bid 3 ♠; and West 4 ♠. Your partner, North, led the ♣ Q, which you took with your ace. What do you lead to trick two? North and South were using primary signals only.

♠ ♡ ◇ ♣ ◇ ♡ ♠ ♡ ◇ ♣ ◇ ♡ ♠

"Poor Mortimer. He just couldn't learn that he shouldn't psyche vulnerable when partnering his wife."

Deal 82 Quiz No Score

West, Dummy	North	East
	♣ 7 K A	
♠ J 7 6 2		
♡ Q J 4		
◇ K 9 4		
♣ 10 6 3		♣ 4 8 J

South, You
♠ Q 4
♡ 6 5 3
◇ A Q J 10 6 3
♣ Q 5

West	North	East	South
—	—	1 ♠	2 ◇
Pass	3 ♣	3 ♡	Pass
4 ♠	Pass	Pass	Pass

You, South, lead the ♣ Q, which wins. Next you lead the ♣ 5, which North wins with king; then North wins the ♣ A and East, the declarer, still follows suit.

You need one more trick to break the contract. Will your ◇ A furnish this vital trick?

The sure way to score your fourth trick is to have your partner lead a fourth club and set up your ♠ Q-4 for an **en passant** trump trick.

So, what do you discard on your partner's ♣ A:

1. If you are playing primary discards only?
2. If playing discard suit-preference signals?

Deal 83 Quiz No Score

North
♠ 6

East, Dummy
♠ J 7 3
♡ K 10 4
♢ K 10 6
♣ A 5 4 2

South, You
♠ K 9 4
♡ 9 7 2
♢ 9 8 5 3
♣ 8 7 6

West opened 2 NT and East made it 6 NT.

North opens the ♠ 6, and dummy injected the seven.

Sitting South, which spade do you play on this trick? Why?

How do you plan your later defense?

SOLUTIONS TO QUIZZES

Deal 43 Solution Ancient Signal 3 ♠ by West

<table>
<tr><td></td><td>♠ 5 3
♡ 10 7 6 5
◇ 9 2
♣ K Q J 9 5</td><td></td></tr>
<tr><td>♠ A K 10 9
♡ 9 4 2
◇ A K J 5
♣ 10 4</td><td></td><td>♠ Q J 8 6
♡ Q 8 3
◇ Q 6 4
♣ 8 7 6</td></tr>
<tr><td></td><td>♠ 7 4 2
♡ A K J
◇ 10 8 7 3
♣ A 3 2</td><td></td></tr>
</table>

South must overtake the ♣ K opening with the ace, lay down the ♡ K which North will read as asking for a heart lead; then South should switch back to a club to North. North returns a heart to let South pick up ♡ Q from dummy and break the contract.

If South errs by playing a low club on the ♣ K opening, North might make a fatal shift to a diamond, a wrong guess, and let declarer get home.

This type of temporary switch is also used to cash a dry (singleton) ace or dry ace-king, preparatory to ruffing.

The ancient signal in this deal is as old as the game of bridge. This signal is a PRIMARY signal because it directs partner to lead the signalling suit itself. Although the signal shows preference, it is not a suit-preference signal by modern definition and absolutely not a Lavinthal.

Deal 44 Solution Black Magic 3 ♡ by East

North:
♠ A Q 5
♡ 9
◇ A K Q 7 5 3
♣ 8 5 3

West:
♠ K J 10 7
♡ Q J 3
◇ 9 6 4
♣ A Q 2

East:
♠ 9 4
♡ A K 7 6 4 2
◇ J 10 8
♣ K 6

South:
♠ 8 6 3 2
♡ 10 8 5
◇ 2
♣ J 10 9 7 4

North won ◇ 2 opening with ace, cashed ◇ Q, then gave South a diamond ruff. Clearly South read North for ◇ A-K-Q, else declarer would have won a diamond trick. And North's unusual play of ◇ A first is a suit-preference signal, asking South to lead the higher ranking of the other two plain suits, a spade. So South led a spade and North won two spade tricks to defeat the contract.

In the duplicate game where this deal occurred, most Souths, not playing SPS's, returned the ♣ J to trick four that let East fulfill his contract. But one South got novel and flipped a coin, saying, "Heads I lead a spade, tails a club." He was a lucky crapshooter, for the coin landed heads up This kind of black magic in the black suits is only a 50% chance whereas a SPS is almost 100% sure.

Deal 45 Solution Blocking 3 NT by East

West	North	East
	♠ J 10 5 2	
	♡ K 10 3	
	◇ Q 6 3	
	♣ K 8 3	
♠ 8 7 4		♠ A K 3
♡ J 7 4		♡ A 9 5
◇ A J 10 9 5		◇ 7 4
♣ 7 4		♣ A Q J 10 5
	♠ Q 9 6	
	♡ Q 8 6 2	
	◇ K 8 2	
	♣ 9 6 2	

South opened the ♡ 2 and East won the third heart lead. On this South should drop his ♡ Q, marked as being originally from a four-card suit. This unnecessarily high card can only be read as a suit-preference signal, directing North to lead the higher ranking of the two unplayed suits, excluding dummy's threatening diamonds. A spade lead was directed, but the SPS was incidental here, for the diamond suit is the vital feature.

When East leads the ◇ 7 to trick four, South should put up the king. This play kills dummy's diamonds if North holds ◇ Q-x-x. Also the immediate ◇ K may induce East to place it as a false card from ◇ K-Q, and so duck. South cashes his heart trick, then leads a diamond. If declarer finesses dummy's ten, North's queen wins and declarer not only gets no diamond trick, but also he loses his chance to take a club finesse.

If South ducks the first diamond lead, dummy inserts

the ◊ 9 and North's queen wins. East wins any return and finesses diamonds to score all the suit. North can kill dummy's diamonds by letting the ◊ 9 win the first diamond lead, but first North would have to consult a voodoo doctor to know that South holds the ◊ K.

Deal 46 Solution Holding Play 4 ♡ by East

North:
♠ J 10 7 6 3 2
♡ 3
◊ 9 7
♣ A 9 8 5

West:
♠ K Q
♡ Q 10 8
◊ K Q 6 5 3
♣ 7 3 2

East:
♠ A 5
♡ K J 9 7 5
◊ A J 10 2
♣ 6 4

South:
♠ 9 8 4
♡ A 6 4 2
◊ 8 4
♣ K Q J 10

South wins ♣ K then ♣ Q, and East ruffs ♣ J. East returns the ♡ 7. If South wins the first or second trump lead, declarer wins any return, draws trumps, and scores game.

South must make a holding play and keep his ♡ A until the third trump lead, so that dummy will have no trump left to ruff a club. Next South must push his club to force East's last trump and so make South's fourth trump "the last of the Mohicans" for the setting trick.

If East leads trumps twice only and shifts to diamonds, South gets a diamond ruff and trump ace to break the contract.

Deal 47 Solution Cheap Camouflage 3 NT by East

♠ 7 6 3
♡ J 10 9 5
◇ 10 4
♣ Q 10 9 4

♠ Q 9 8 5 2
♡ 8 4 3
◇ A 9
♣ A K J

♠ A 4
♡ A K 6 2
◇ K 6 3
♣ 8 7 6 2

♠ K J 10
♡ Q 7
◇ Q J 8 7 5 2
♣ 5 3

South leads ◇ 7 to ace in dummy. Next ♠ 2 goes to East's ace, and South's best play is the ♠ K! This play must be made quickly and smoothly lest East suspect South of his gigantic false card. Placing ♠ J-10-7-6-3 in North, most likely declarer will quit the apparently hopeless spade suit fast and look for greener pastures in the heart and club suits. These break badly so declarer will probably fail to go game with ten tricks frigid.

South's ♠ K false card is not even a gambit, for South always has one natural spade stopper however he elects to play his spades. It is cheap camouflage.

When you lack the brute force to defeat a contract, try larceny. In bridge it can pay off.

Deal 48 Solution Deschapelles Coup 3 NT by West

West	North / South	East
	♠ 10 9 8 5 ♡ K Q J 10 5 3 ◇ — ♣ Q 7 4	
♠ 6 ♡ A 6 4 ◇ A K Q 6 4 ♣ 10 9 8 6		♠ A K J 7 ♡ 9 8 7 ◇ 8 7 5 3 ♣ A J
	♠ Q 4 3 2 ♡ 2 ◇ J 10 9 2 ♣ K 5 3 2	

North led ♡ K then ♡ 10 to West's ♡ A. West cashed ◇ A, ◇ K then lost ◇ 4 to South. South can count declarer for eight cold tricks, ♡ A, ♠ A-K, ♣ A and four diamond tricks. If West holds the ♣ Q, stopping game is hopeless, so South must lay down the ♣ K, the famous Deschapelles Coup.

In the actual game, dummy won the ♣ K with ♣ A. Declarer placed South with the ♣ Q, and returned a club at once to set up the game-going trick in clubs. But North grabbed ♣ J with the ♣ Q and ran his great heart suit to set the contract three tricks!

Deal 49 Solution Double Lavinthal 4 ♡ by East

West	North	East
	♠ 9 8 5 4	
	♡ 6 2	
	◇ K 7 6 2	
	♣ 10 7 2	
♠ Q 7 3		♠ J 2
♡ K Q 8 3		♡ A J 10 9 7
◇ 10 9 3		◇ Q 8 4
♣ 6 5 3		♣ A K Q
	♠ A K 10 6	
	♡ 5 4	
	◇ A J 5	
	♣ J 9 8 4	

South led ♠ K. He saw the discouraging ♠ 4 drop from North and the menacing ♠ Q in dummy. A shift was urgent. So South, right or wrong and like a little old lady in doubt, shifted to a trump, the ♡ 5. This card was worthless trick-wise yet could signify a side suit that South wanted led. **North attached no significance to the ♡ 5 until declarer drew** South's second trump, the ♡ 4. This high-low play implied suit-preference to North, for the higher-ranking of the other two plain suits, diamonds. North, who viewed his hand as practically worthless, now realized the potent value of his ◇ K.

To trick three East led ♠ J to set up dummy's ♠ Q for a diamond discard later, South won with his ♠ A and saw North follow with the NINE of spades.

This was clearly suit-preference. South read the ♠ 9 and made the "mad" lead of the ◇ 5 away from ◇ A-J-5. North won the ◇ 5 with his king and returned a diamond to let South score ◇ A-J for two more tricks, setting declarer one.

Deal 50 Solution Counter Gambit 4 ♠ by West

	North	
	♠ — ♡ A 9 7 6 5 ◇ Q J 10 9 7 ♣ 10 8 6	
♠ A K J 10 9 8 6 4 ♡ Q J ◇ — ♣ A Q 7		♠ 7 2 ♡ 10 8 2 ◇ 8 6 3 2 ♣ 9 5 4 2
	♠ Q 5 3 ♡ K 4 3 ◇ A K 5 4 ♣ K J 3	

West ruffs ◇ Q, S wins ♡ K, West ruffs ◇ K, North wins ♡ A, and West ruffs ◇ J. To trick six declarer leads ♠ J on which North discards ♡ 6.

South counts West for eight spades, two hearts, no diamond, and three unknown cards. West's 2 ♠ opening shows ♣ A-Q, for South is looking at ♣ K-J-3. This leaves one card in doubt.

If West held a third heart, he would lead a top trump first early instead of pushing hearts then donating ♠ J to ♠ Q in order to make ♠ 7 an entry to dummy. This one-trick gambit will let dummy in to score ♡ 10 then let West finesse ♣ Q to win. In exchange, West will get TWO tricks as his payoff.

South's counter gambit is to let that ♠ J win!

Deal 51 Solution Blackmail 3 NT by West

	North	
	♠ Q 5 3 ♡ Q 8 4 ◇ J 9 8 4 3 ♣ 3 2	
♠ K 9 8 ♡ K 9 5 2 ◇ K 10 5 ♣ 9 7 6		♠ A J 7 ♡ A 10 ◇ 7 2 ♣ A Q J 10 8 4
	♠ 10 6 4 2 ♡ J 7 6 3 ◇ A Q 6 ♣ K 5	

North leads the ◇ 4 and South should play the QUEEN. This standard play blackmails West to take his ◇ K at once. If West holds up, the grave danger is a return through the ◇ K which is fatal if North holds the ◇ A. Declarer must live on clubs and so he finesses a club to trick two. South wins his ♣ K, then cashes ◇ A and leads another diamond; so his side gets more tricks to defeat the contract.

As the cards lie, the ◇ K holdup at trick one is a winning play, even if West guesses wrong on a low diamond return; but this is double dummy strictly for the autopsy birds.

If South plays his ◇ A to trick one, West has no problem and simply holds up his ◇ K until the third diamond lead.

Deal 52 Solution No High-Low 4 ♡ by West

West	North	East
	♠ 10 7 4 2	
	♡ —	
	◇ A K 5 4	
	♣ Q 6 5 3 2	
♠ 8 5		♠ A Q 9
♡ A K 8 6 4 3		♡ J 7 5 2
◇ Q 7 6		◇ J 10 9 2
♣ A K		♣ 9 7
	♠ K J 6 3	
	♡ Q 10 9	
	◇ 8 3	
	♣ J 10 8 4	

North opens the ◇ K and South should play the ◇ 3. South should not signal high low because a ruff which spends a natural trump trick gains nothing. South's one chance to gain a trick is in spades. The discouraging ◇ 3 play should induce North to switch to a spade, thus netting the setting trick.

If South plays the ◇ 8 to trick one, North next will cash the ◇ A then give his partner a diamond ruff. But the defence runs out of gas. Declarer will get in, draw trumps, and discard a spade on the fourth diamond.

Deal 53 Solution Trapped East in 1 ♠ Doubled

	North	
	♠ Q J 10 9 8 ♡ Q 10 9 ♢ 10 5 2 ♣ 8 4	
♠ 4 3 ♡ J 8 5 2 ♢ J 9 7 3 ♣ 10 5 2		♠ A 7 6 5 2 ♡ 6 3 ♢ 8 4 ♣ A K 7 3
	♠ K ♡ A K 7 4 ♢ A K Q 6 ♣ Q J 9 6	

South should open the ♠ K! North showed great trump strength by his penalty pass to the takeout double. Actually, North's penalty pass was skimpy, but his ♡ Q looked like a key card as the takeout double suggested heart strength. Declarer let the ♠ K win. South next laid down ♡ K, then a low ♡ that North's ♡ 9 won. North led the ♠ Q and East won with the ♠ A. East should have cashed his top clubs now, but instead he led a low diamond, hoping to ruff a diamond later. South boldly ducked, dummy finessed the ♢ 9 and North won with the ten! North drew trumps in three leads on which South parked his clubs, so North-South won 12 tricks!

Deal 54 Solution Blackwood Barred 6 ◇ by East

Kenneth Konstam, world championship contender and bridge editor of the **London Sunday Times,** cited Sam Fry Jr. an Oscar for one of the best played hands of the year, shown below. Fry played it in the staid British Portland Club, noted since 1930 for its adverse view on artificial bids and wholesale ace-showing conventions. Realizing this, Fry by-passed the Blackwood 4 NT Convention and jumped directly to 6 ◇, only to find that he was off two aces.

However, I doubt if the Portland Club would object to such conventions of play as the come-on and suit-preference signals.

	♠ A 10 5 4 ♡ Q 10 9 ◇ 4 2 ♣ J 10 9 3	
♠ 9 8 3 ♡ J 5 4 2 ◇ A K ♣ K Q 7 6		♠ K Q 6 2 ♡ A ◇ Q J 10 9 8 7 6 ♣ 4
	♠ J 7 ♡ K 8 7 6 3 ◇ 5 3 ♣ A 8 5 2	

South opened ◇ 5 to ◇ K. East won ♠ K on trick two; then East returned the club that South won with his ace.

Not suspecting ♠ A in North, South led another diamond

to ace, and dummy was on lead for the last time. Fry could have played safe for one down by cashing dummy's top clubs for two spade discards. But Fry preferred a chance, however slim, for the grand prize. So instead he came to hand via ♡ A and ran all his diamonds. On trick ten North, down to ♠ A and ♣ J-10-9, thought that he was squeezed. A club discard looked fatal, so North gambled that his partner held ♠ Q. North let go the ♠ A, and Fry blithely cashed three spade tricks for his brilliantly earned slam, — and his prized Oscar.

But Fry would have had no chance against good defensive carding. When south wins trick three with ♣ A, North should play the JACK OF CLUBS. South would wonder why declarer failed to draw the last trump, then would realize that declarer dared not lest North make a revealing discard. What proved that North's ♣ J play was not forced was declarer's haste to lead a club. If declarer held four clubs, he would not risk a club lead before drawing trumps. So North's unnecessarily high ♣ J play must be a suit-preference signal. It would direct the lead of the higher-ranking of the other two plain suits, a spade. So South would lead a spade to North's ace to set declarer.

And North would not sit back and call it a day. Bridge players are naturally greedy souls, and rightly so if they are to win the maximum. North would have noted that South had followed suit with the ♠ 7 then had led ♠ J. This would place ♠ Q with East,, and if the ♠ 7 was South's lowest, South was fresh out of spades. So North would return a spade to let South get a ruff for the second setting trick.

Albert H. Morehead reported the deal in the **New York Times** of 8 January 1962.

Grand larceny like Fry's is fun, especially when it nets an impossible slam plus two Oscars, the second by Morehead, to frost the cake.

Deal 55 Solution Control 4 ♡ by West

	♠ K 4 2 ♡ 5 4 2 ◇ K Q 6 4 ♣ 9 4 2	
♠ 9 8 7 ♡ Q J 9 7 6 3 ◇ 10 ♣ A Q 6		♠ J 5 ♡ K 10 ◇ A 9 8 5 2 ♣ K J 8 5
	♠ A Q 10 6 3 ♡ A 8 ◇ J 7 3 ♣ 10 7 3	

Bridge writers usually suppress hands which they have misplayed, or fiction the result to their favor. However we admit to missing the killing defense agains 4 ♡. Declarer probably holds three low spades, and he must not be allowed to ruff any in dummy. South must overtake ♠ K with ace. But it is futile to switch to ♡ A then ♡ 8, for if West has ♣ A-x-x, he enters his own hand via ♣ A, draws trumps, then parks his third spade on dummy's fourth club.

To trick two South must lead the ♡ 8! This play ties declarer in knots. If he leads another spade, South wins it, draws dummy's last trump, and breaks the contract with the third spade trick.

Deal 56 Solution Plan to Ruff 4 ♡ by West

	North	
	♠ 9 6 2 ♡ A ◇ K J 9 4 2 ♣ Q 10 8 4	
♠ J 5 3 ♡ K J 8 7 5 ◇ A 8 5 ♣ K 7		♠ A K ♡ Q 10 9 4 ◇ Q 10 3 ♣ J 9 6 3
	♠ Q 10 8 7 4 ♡ 6 3 2 ◇ 7 6 ♣ A 5 2	

South wins North's ♣ 4 opening with his ace. Clubs offer no more nourishment if South continues them. Even if North holds the ♣ K and West the ♣ Q, another club lead will set up dummy's jack. Trumps and spades are hopeless, so South's best return is the ◇ 7. Whether West wins now or ducks, North gets in later with the trump ace to cash the ◇ K (if not previously made) and lets South ruff a diamond to set the contract one trick.

Of course, if West ducks the diamond lead to North's king, North must lead another diamond at once.

Deal 57 Solution Re-affirmed 3 NT by East

♠ A 7 4
♡ A K 10 8 3 2
◇ 9 4
♣ 5 4

♠ Q 10 6
♡ 9 6
◇ K 5 3
♣ A 9 8 6 3

♠ K J
♡ Q 7 5 4
◇ A Q J 2
♣ K J 7

♠ 9 8 5 3 2
♡ J
◇ 10 8 7 6
♣ Q 10 2

North wins the ♡ J with his ♡ A, wins ♡ K, then loses ♡ 10 to queen. Declarer cashes ♣ A then loses ♣ J finesse to South's queen while North echoes ♣ 5 then ♣ 4.

South should lead a spade. North scored his ♡ A before his ♡ K, an unusual play as an unusual suit-preference signal, directing South to lead the higher ranking suit, a spade. The club suit is obviously excluded from choice as it is declarer's running suit. Also, North reaffirmed his spade entry by his club echo, an emphatic repeat SPS.

Deal 58 Solution Too Many Trumps 4 ♠ by East

	♠ 6 ♡ 8 5 4 3 2 ◇ 9 7 4 2 ♣ A 5 2	
♠ A Q J ♡ Q J 10 ◇ K J 5 3 ♣ K 6 3		♠ K 9 8 5 3 ♡ A K 9 6 ◇ Q 10 ♣ 7 4
	♠ 10 7 4 2 ♡ 7 ◇ A 8 6 ♣ Q J 10 9 8	

East ruffed the third club lead and he led the ◇ 10. South must step up the ◇ A and lead another club! This play is normally improper because of the hope that declarer will let the ◇ 10 ride to your partner's queen. Two facts favor taking the ◇ A immediately. First it is unlikely that your partner holds the ◇ Q. You can account for 11 high-card points held by your side. Dummy shows 17 points. With 40 points in the pack, would it be too much to expect the opening bidder to hold 12 points? Second, you can set the contract if you can force declarer down to a shorter trump length than your own, leaving you in control with too many trumps for declarer's comfort.

After taking the ◇ A, you should lead a club. While this appears to violate another principle against giving declarer a ruff and discard, you know that he has no loser in his plain suits which he could discard to profit.

If you duck the ◇ 10, declarer sneaks home a diamond trick, wins three trumps in dummy, takes the ♡ A, draws your last trump, and scores three more heart tricks for game.

Deal 59 Solution Jo College 4 ♠ by West

West	North	East
	♠ 9 4 2	
	♡ K 9 5 4	
	◇ 7	
	♣ J 8 6 4 2	
♠ K J 10 6 5 3		♠ A Q 7
♡ J		♡ Q 8 3
◇ K 8 6		◇ Q J 10 4 3
♣ A 10 3		♣ K 9
	♠ 8	
	♡ A 10 7 6 2	
	◇ A 9 5 2	
	♣ Q 7 5	

North led the ◇ 7 which South won with the ◇ A and West falsecarded his eightspot. Despite this South must read that ◇ 7 opening as a singleton. South should return his best diamond, the nine, as a suit-preference signal directing a heart lead. North ruffs the ◇ 9, returns a low heart to South's ♡ A and South gives North another diamond ruff to break the contract.

In this Deal No. 16 of the 1962 Intercollegiate Championships, the trap contract is 3 NT by East. South opens the ♡ 6 and his side gets five heart tricks plus the ◇ A to set the contract two tricks. The 4 ♠ contract is superior because West's 1 ♠ opening is based chiefy on shape and also 4 ♠ can be defeated only one trick.

Deal 60 Solution Fast Play 3 NT by West

	North	
	♠ 10 8 6 4 ♡ 5 3 ◇ 9 8 6 3 ♣ J 9 2	
♠ J 9 2 ♡ A 7 4 ◇ K Q 5 ♣ 10 7 6 4		♠ K Q 7 ♡ Q 9 6 ◇ J 10 2 ♣ A K Q 3
	♠ A 5 3 ♡ K J 10 8 2 ◇ A 7 4 ♣ 8 5	

North leads ♡ 5 to ♡ 8 and ace. West leads ♣ 4 to queen, then dummy leads ◇ J. South must step up with ◇ A at once then clear his heart suit fast. This lets dummy's ♡ Q score but declarer has only eight tricks, two hearts, two diamonds and four clubs. He needs a spade trick, but South wins the first spade lead and scores three heart tricks to break the contract.

In the actual game, South ducked the ◇ J lead "to let partner make ◇ Q and lead another heart." This is what declarer was fishing for, so he shifted to a spade that South won. But it was too late.

If West holds ◇ K-Q-x-x, no defense stops game; if ◇ K-x-x, any defense stops game; if ◇ K-9-x-x, North's ◇ Q always scores.

Deal 61 Solution Do It Yourself 5 ♣ by West

	North	
	♠ J 7 6 5 4 2 ♡ K Q 10 6 ◇ 10 9 6 ♣ —	
♠ A 9 ♡ 7 ◇ A Q 2 ♣ Q J 10 8 7 5 2		♠ 10 3 ♡ 9 4 2 ◇ K J 8 5 ♣ K 9 6 4
	♠ K Q 8 ♡ A J 8 5 3 ◇ 7 4 3 ♣ A 3	

On North's opening ♡ K lead, South could play the ♡ J as a suit-preference signal. It would suggest that North switch to the higher-ranking plain suit, a spade. Time is urgent and South knows that the setting trick must be set up and won before declarer drives out the ♣ A, draws trump and parks any spade loser or losers that he may have on dummy's diamond suit.

Rather than trust partner to switch to a spade, South should overtake the ♡ K with the ace and lead the ♠ K.

On defense bear in mind that a signal should be given only when partner's co-operation is essential. Don't signal partner to do something that you can do yourself. Partner could err if you ask him to do your work for you.

Beware! A second heart lead (unlikely on the auction) should not be risked until the spade trick has been won.

Deal 62 Solution Unblock 4 ♠ by East

	North	
	♠ 6 ♡ 6 5 2 ◇ 10 8 7 3 ♣ 9 7 6 4 2	
♠ K J 7 3 ♡ 8 7 4 3 ◇ K 5 4 ♣ 8 5		♠ A Q 10 9 5 2 ♡ J 10 ◇ A 6 2 ♣ A Q
	♠ 8 4 ♡ A K Q 9 ◇ Q J 9 ♣ K J 10 3	

When East lays down the ◇ A at trick seven, South's hand is stripped of both spades and hearts. In order to avoid being endplayed, South, on the ◇ A, must play the ◇ J; then on the ◇ K ditch the ◇ Q to complete the unblock. This lets North win the third diamond lead so as to return a club and promote the setting trick.

Declarer played without forethought. To trick four he should lead a low diamond to dummy's king, making South's unblock more difficult to find. Prematurely declarer's plan became obvious to South especially when North's first discard was his bottom club, drawing attention to the only honor in his hand, the ◇ 10.

Deal 63 Solution Economy 3 NT by West

West	North	East
	♠ A 6 5 2 ♡ 7 4 ◇ 8 5 ♣ 10 9 8 7 5	
♠ K 10 ♡ A Q J ◇ 9 7 4 2 ♣ Q 6 4 3		♠ Q J 9 ♡ K 10 9 8 ◇ K 10 6 ♣ K J 2
	♠ 8 7 4 3 ♡ 6 5 3 2 ◇ A Q J 3 ♣ A	

Against 3 NT North opens the ♣ 10, dummy ducks, and you have to win with your dry ace.

If you shift to the ◇ Q, West's nine will come to a trick. The Summertime ◇ Q lead can be a winning play only if West holds three or fewer diamonds.

The right lead to trick two is the ◇ 3. This is for the proper economy of your diamond honors. You should aim not so much to drive out the ◇ K from dummy but to be able to score later three quick diamond tricks when your partner gets in and returns a diamond through dummy's then doubleton ◇ K.

The ◇ 3 loses to the ◇ 10. With eight tricks on top declarer needs his ninth from spades. So he leads a low spade to his ♠10 and North should step in with his ace and shift to his diamond to defeat the contract.

At double dummy North can defeat the contract by opening a diamond, but why should he?

Deal 64 Solution Ruff and Sluff 6 ♠ by East

	North	
	♠ 7 4 ♡ Q 9 8 6 4 ◇ 6 5 3 2 ♣ Q 6	
♠ K J 10 6 ♡ A 7 5 ◇ J 7 ♣ K 9 7 5		♠ A Q 9 8 3 ♡ K 3 ◇ A 4 ♣ A 10 8 3
	♠ 5 2 ♡ J 10 2 ◇ K Q 10 9 8 ♣ J 4 2	

East won ◇ A, two trumps, ruffed third heart lead, then lost his last diamond to South's queen.

Declarer's play showed two hearts and five spades, so six cards in the minors. East suggested four clubs when he raised West's 1 ♣ bid, and so East's diamond throw-in play looks as if he lacked the ♣ Q and he is trying to coax South to open clubs. If South co-operates, East picks up ♣ Q then later finesses through South's ♣ J to bring home the slam.

South's best defense is to return the ◇ 10, giving declarer a ruff and discard yet making him keep a club loser. If East has only three clubs, the diamond return does him no good, for he will have a diamond left in his hand.

Deal 65 Solution Trump "Discard" 5 ♡ by West

	♠ A K J 10 8 6 5 ♡ A ◇ 8 3 2 ♣ 7 3	
♠ 3 ♡ K Q J 10 8 6 ◇ 7 6 5 ♣ 9 8 4		♠ 9 7 4 2 ♡ 7 4 ◇ A K 9 ♣ A K Q 6
	♠ Q ♡ 9 5 3 2 ◇ Q J 10 4 ♣ J 10 5 2	

North wins ♠ K. N leads ♠ A on which South discards ◇ 4 and West ruffs. West loses ♡ 10 to North's ♡ A. Next North leads his good ♠ J which South must TRUMP LOW. South, who is momentarily squeezed in the minor suits, must "discard" a low trump. West ruffs and runs trumps. His last trump lead squeezes dummy before South, and South simply discards from the same suit that dummy does in order to realize the setting trick.

Usually a defender keeps his trumps, but here they are useless. The weak 2 ♡ opening marks West with a six-card suit headed by ♡ K-Q-J-10 for his minimum of 6 points with no possible other high-card point count in his hand.

Deal 66 Solution The Unusual Ten 2 NT by West

West		East
	♠ Q 5 4 ♡ K Q J 10 9 3 ◇ 5 ♣ K J 7	
♠ A 8 3 ♡ A 7 5 ◇ 7 6 3 ♣ A 9 6 5		♠ K J 7 ♡ 6 ◇ A K J 9 4 ♣ 10 8 4 2
	♠ 10 9 6 2 ♡ 8 4 2 ◇ Q 10 8 2 ♣ Q 3	

North, before leading, looked for a side-suit entry tc bring in his great heart suit after the ♡ A was driven out. His ♣ K-J-7 offered hope, so he made the unusual ♡ 10 lead from his quart minor K-Q-J-10, relying on declarer to hold up the ♡ A once to let North lead another heart at once to clarify his sequence. Next North led the ♡ K which also won, then North lost the ♡ Q to West's ♡ A.

The unusual ♡ 10 lead was an unusual suit-preference signal, directing South to lead the lowest-ranking suit, a club. So when South won a diamond finesse, he led the ♣ Q and eventually set declarer one trick.

In the other room where North opened the ♡ K normally, South, on winning the diamond finesse, led a spade to North's hoped-for ace. This gave declarer time to set up and score his fifth diamond and make 2 NT.

If North holds ♡ K-Q-J-x-x x (without the ten), he can direct a club lead by opening the jack. South, when in with the ◇ Q, would recognize the SPS and would lead the lower ranking of his other two remaining suits, a club.

Compare this deal with deals 30 and 42.

Deal 67 Solution Dry Ace 3 NT by East

♠ 4 3
♡ 7 6 2
◇ K 8 7 2
♣ 7 6 4 2

West	East
♠ A	♠ Q 8 6 5
♡ 9 3	♡ A K J 8 5
◇ A 9 4 3	◇ Q J 10
♣ Q J 10 9 8 3	♣ A

♠ K J 10 9 7 2
♡ Q 10 4
◇ 6 5
♣ K 5

South led ♠ J to dummy's ace. East finessed ♡ J to South's queen. Let us count East's hand.

To open 1 ♡ then to say 3 NT, East must hold:

♠ Q-x-x-x-? ♡ A-K-J-? ◇ Q-J-? ♣ A-?

East FAILED to attack dummy's great club suit, marking ♣ A a singleton! East's two cards in question must be two diamonds or a diamond and a heart.

If East holds ◇ K-Q-x, 3 NT is back to back; so North must hold ◇ K to give the defense a chance.

The defenders need five tricks to set the contract, ♡ Q, ◇ K, two spades, and the KING OF CLUBS.

At trick three South must avoid the error of leading a diamond, because East can live on diamonds after the ◇ K is gone. Instead, to trick three South must lead the ♣ 5 to drop the dry ace!

Deal 68 Solution False Ace 3 NT by West

West	North	East
	♠ 7 3 2	
	♡ J 10 8 3	
	◇ 9 4 2	
	♣ Q 6 3	
♠ 10 9 5		♠ K J 8 4
♡ A K 7 4		♡ Q 9 5
◇ K J 7		◇ 6 5
♣ K 7 4		♣ A J 9 2
	♠ A Q 6	
	♡ 6 2	
	◇ A Q 10 8 3	
	♣ 10 8 5	

North opens the ◇ 9 and West is allowed to win it with the jack. Next West finesses the ♠ 10.

If South wins with ♠ Q and drives out West's ◇ K, South's good diamonds with ♠ A still at large will push West into a new plan, — to finesse clubs and run them for four tricks.

South should paint a false picture in spades and keep West happy, — until it is too late. South should win trick two with the ♠ A! Next South establishes his diamonds. West, confident that ♠ Q is in North, will finesse another spade to South's ♠ Q and let South run diamonds.

If West smells fish and cashes three top hearts first, South should not give away the show by a club discard. Instead he should make his ♠ A false card look really genuine by discarding the ♠ 6!

Deal 69 Solution Scuttle 3 NT by East

♠ K Q 9 8 2
♡ J 4 2
◇ 9 7 2
♣ 10 6

♠ A 5
♡ 8 3
◇ 8 6 4 3
♣ 9 5 4 3 2

♠ J 10 7 3
♡ A K Q 5
◇ A 5
♣ A Q J

♠ 6 4
♡ 10 9 7 6
◇ K Q J 10
♣ K 8 7

South opened ◇ K to East's ace. East led ♣ A then ♣ Q. This South must win at once with ♣ K and switch IMMEDIATELY to ♠ 6 in an effort to scuttle dummy's only entry, the ♠ A, before clubs are unblocked. South, seeing that the long club suit is declarer's salvation, must make every effor to keep clubs blocked.

South cannot cash diamond tricks before leading a spade lest East jettison his blocking ♣ J. South can cash his diamonds later. They will keep.

A clever East might lead the ♣ J to trick two and I bet dollars to doughnuts that South would duck. And with a smile from ear to ear declarer would next lay down the ♣ A then ♣ Q to clear his suit.

Deal 70 Solution Catch a Thief 3 NT by East

♠ 6 5 2
♡ 9 8 7
◇ A J 8 2
♣ 6 5 4

♠ 4
♡ Q 5
◇ Q 9 7 5
♣ K Q 10 8 7 3

♠ A K 7
♡ K J 10 4 2
◇ 6 3
♣ A J 9

♠ Q J 10 9 8 3
♡ A 6 3
◇ K 10 4
♣ 2

South leads ♠ Q to East's ♠ A. East returns ♡ 2.

East persisted to 3 NT over West's 3 ♣ signoff because East holds at least ♣ A-x. South must spot East's planned larceny, to conceal eight running tricks in clubs and ♠ A-K until East has filched a heart trick before defenders get on to him.

South must win trick two with the ♡ A.

Only diamonds show promise of defeating the contract. South must hope for ◇ A-J-8-x in North.

If South leds ◇ K then ◇ 10, dummy covers with ◇ Q to stop diamonds with the ◇ 9. So to trick three South must lead the TEN of diamonds. Queen and ace cover. Back comes a diamond to king, then South leads ◇ 4 thru ◇ 9-7 toward North's ◇ J-8. Thus can South catch a thief.

Deal 71 Solution Double Holdup 4 ♡ by West

West	North	East
	♠ K Q J 6 2	
	♡ 9 6	
	◇ Q 10 7 4	
	♣ 8 2	
♠ A 10		♠ 9 7
♡ Q J 10 4 3		♡ K 8 5
◇ A K J		◇ 8 5 2
♣ 9 7 3		♣ K Q J 10 5
	♠ 8 5 4 3	
	♡ A 7 2	
	◇ 9 6 3	
	♣ A 6 4	

North leads the ♠ K to West's ace. West returns the ♡ Q which South must let win. If West returns another heart,* South should take his ace and return the third heart.

This play kill's dummy's only entry to cash in on the great club suit. When West leads clubs, North should echo with the ♣ 8 then ♣ 2 to show two clubs and so let South know that West holds three clubs. South will know that he must hold up the ♣ A until the third club lead.

Having no entry to clubs, West must try the ◇ J finesse and go down one.

If South wins trick three with the ♡ A and fails to return a heart, later West drives out South's ♣ A and makes 4 ♡. As soon as West gets in, he crosses to dummy via the ♡ K and runs two clubs for discards.

Cook: South can hold up his ♡ A twice to make game.

---

*To trick three West should first lay down the ◇ A, then lead a heart, as a safety play preparatory to a diamond finesse later if needed. **Editor.**

Deal 72 Solution Royal Signal 3 NT by East

West	North	East
	♠ 9 7 5 4 2	
	♡ J 10 5	
	◇ 10 8 5	
	♣ K 4	
♠ K		♠ Q J 10 3
♡ 9 3 2		♡ A 7 6
◇ 9 7 4 2		◇ A K Q
♣ A Q J 6 2		♣ 10 7 3
	♠ A 8 6	
	♡ K Q 8 4	
	◇ J 6 3	
	♣ 9 8 5	

South opened the ♡ 4 and North scored his ten then jack. East's ♡ A won the third heart lead and on this South should play his KING, a royal signal. Clearly North can read South for the ♡ Q also, otherwise declarer would have taken trick one with the queen. With hearts exhausted from all hands but South's, the ♡ K can only be read as a suit-preference signal, directing the lead of the higher ranking of the two remaining suits, a spade, excluding declarer's obvious running club suit. When declarer loses the ♣ 10 finesse to North's king, North leads a spade. South scores the ♠ A, then his lone ♡ Q takes the setting trick.

Without use of the SPS signal, North, when in with the ♣ K and having noted declarer's spade bid bolstered by the ♠ K in dummy, will naturally lead a diamond up to dummy's weakness. This would let declarer score nine tricks before spades are touched.

Deal 73 Solution Judgment 5 ♠ by East

As they say, "The exception proves the rule." While a suit-preference signal is a command to lead a specified suit, this command does not transcend good judgment. The deal below from a duplicate game illustrates the point, despite the fact that casual players not playing SPS's can set 5 ♠.

West	North	East
	♠ 8 4	
	♡ Q J 9 5	
	◇ A 9 3 2	
	♣ 9 7 6	
♠ A 10 6 2		♠ K Q J 9 5
♡ 8		♡ 7 4 2
◇ K Q 5 4		◇ J 10 8
♣ A J 10 2		♣ 8 3
	♠ 7 3	
	♡ A K 10 6 3	
	◇ 7 6	
	♣ K Q 5 4	

South opened the ♡ K and North played the ♡ J as a SPS, directing a diamond switch. Despite this command South should use his judgement and instead to trick two lead the ♣ K. North's ◇ A can wait, even if North holds ◇ A-J-10. It is vital for South to use his tempo to set up and score his club trick lest declarer hold only two clubs and eventually discard one on the fourth diamond trick.

Compare with Deal 61, Do It Yourself, and Deal 79, Preferred Practice.

Deal 74 Solution Tempo 5 ♣ by East

	North	
	♠ 4 3 ♡ Q 10 6 2 ◇ 10 9 6 4 3 ♣ 6 3	
♠ K Q 8 7 5 2 ♡ K 8 4 ◇ 5 2 ♣ 9 5		♠ J 10 9 ♡ A 5 3 ◇ A ♣ A Q J 10 8 4
	♠ A 6 ♡ J 9 7 ◇ K Q J 8 7 ♣ K 7 2	

The auction is poor, as 4 ♠ is cold, or 6 ♠ if North holds ♣ K. But the point is defense to 5 ♣.

Tempo is urgent. With two stoppers, ♣ K and ♠ A, South must open hearts at once to develop a possible third-round heart trick while the diamond suit can wait once. South can afford a futile heart opening and shift to diamonds in time, — but not vice versa.

Also South's own strength plus East's strong bidding revealed North with little but many diamonds for his 2 ◇ raise. A defense trick in diamonds is nearly hopeless.

The mechanical ◇ K opening gives declarer time to drive out both ♣ K and ♠ A, then to park his heart loser on dummy's great spade suit.

Deal 75 Solution Double Tenace 3 NT by West

North:
♠ 7 5
♡ 9 6 5
◇ J 10 9 4 2
♣ Q 10 4

West:
♠ 8 4 2
♡ K J 7
◇ Q 6
♣ A K 8 7 5

East:
♠ K J 3
♡ A Q 8
◇ A 7 3
♣ 9 6 3 2

South:
♠ A Q 10 9 6
♡ 10 4 3 2
◇ K 8 5
♣ J

North opens the ◇ J and it rides to South's king. South sees no future in diamonds and he has his own worthwhile suit, so he leads the TEN OF SPADES that dummy's ♠ J wins. South made the right lead from his double tenace.

West leads a club off dummy, planning to make a safety duck if South produces the queen, dry or otherwise. But South's ♣ J ruins this chance, so West plays ♣ A-K, hoping to find two or fewer clubs in North. Clubs split badly, so West creams his eight tricks off the top, settling for one down.

At other tables West made 3 NT because South to trick two made the WRONG LEAD from his double tenace, the QUEEN of spades. This was an omen of trouble, so dummy could, and did, lay off as a standard holdup play while promoting a sure spade stopper. Next South led a low spade to dummy. But this milked North dry of spades and he had none to return when he won the third club lead.

Deal 76 Solution Contra Squeeze 5 ♢ by West

West	North	East
	♠ K Q 8 7 4 2	
	♡ 10 9 7 5	
	♢ 2	
	♣ 7 3	
♠ J 9		♠ A 10
♡ J 3		♡ A 4 2
♢ K J 10 9 6 5		♢ Q 8 7 4
♣ A Q 5		♣ K 6 4 2
	♠ 6 5 3	
	♡ K Q 8 6	
	♢ A 3	
	♣ J 10 9 8	

North led ♠ K to ace, and South won the second diamond lead with ♢ A. South returned a spade to North's queen, then North led a heart, but it was too late. Dummy's ♡ A won and declarer ran all his trumps and ♣ A-Q, catching South in an automatic squeeze.

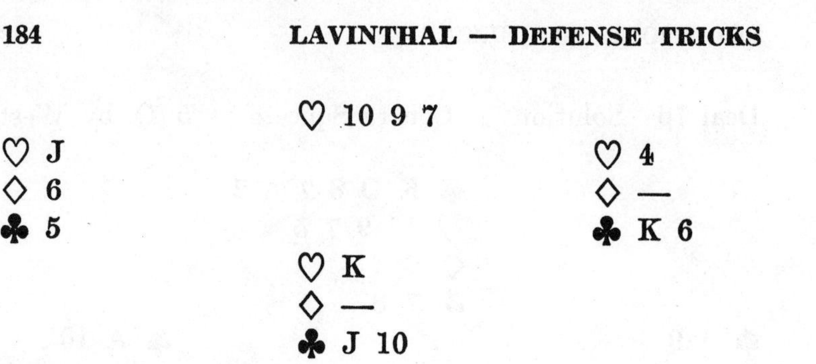

West led his last diamond and pitched the heart from dummy. If South sheds ♡ K, West's ♡ J scores then ♣ K in dummy. If South instead sheds a club, dummy gets the last two tricks in clubs.

At trick four the spade returned looked natural to South, but it let West score his diamond game by the squeeze above.

The defense against this squeeze is for South to let his side keep the spade trick. It will not evaporate. To trick four South must lead his ♡ K to dummy's ace. Add one spade card to each hand in the diagram above and note what happens on West's last diamond lead. South gracefully escapes the squeeze by discarding his last spade.

Deal 77 Solution 77 Sunset Strip 2 ♠ by East

North was chicken for not mentioning his diamond seven-timer with two aces, despite being vulnerable. If North says 2 ◇ over West's 1 NT, South can lift to 3 ◇ over 2 ♠. Or instead North can wait, then balance at 3 ◇ after the auction dies at 2 ♠. Careful play makes 3 ◇ on a coup ending, and East loses all the points if he persists to 3 ♠. But our main interest is defending against 2 ♠.

Deal 77 Solution (Continued from page 184)

West	North	East
	♠ J 6	
	♡ A 7 4	
	◇ J 7 6 5 4 3 2	
	♣ A	
♠ 10 3		♠ A K Q 7 5 4
♡ 10 9 3 2		♡ 8 6 5
◇ K Q 10 8		◇ —
♣ J 8 7		♣ Q 10 9 6
	♠ 9 8 2	
	♡ K Q J	
	◇ A 9	
	♣ K 5 4 3 2	

You need no private eye from 77 Sunset Strip to count East's hand. East played three hearts, showed ♣ Q-10-9-6, rebid spades on five, so has at most one diamond.

At most tables the play went the same at 2 ♠, South tried to take trick seven with the ◇ A, but East ruffed. East drew trumps and claimed for down one for a good score.

To trick seven South must lead a fourth club to let North overruff dummy with a trump picture if held. What happens on the club lead is irrevalent, immaterial and of no consequence to the safety of the ◇ A. It can wait, — always makes if East has a diamond.

North's ◇ 2 discard on the ♣ K at trick six was a discard suit-preference signal, directing South to lead the lower ranking of the other two plain suits, a club. This is probably beyond the 77 Sunset Strip people unless they are bridge experts. Yet South does not need this crutch in this case if he takes the trouble to count thirteen and analyze.

Deal 78 Solution Fatal Force 4 ♠ by West

In match-point duplicate the defenders do not always have to break the contract to earn a top score. If they can hold declarer to ten tricks in a major-suit game for example while all other declarers win extra tricks, the defenders will win all the comparisons for a top score. The next deal shows how a suit-preference signal produced a top-score defense.

West	North	East
	♠ 3	
	♡ A J 9 6 2	
	◇ K 10 9 7 2	
	♣ K J	
♠ 10 9 8 7 5 4		♠ A K Q
♡ 7		♡ K 5 4
◇ Q J 6 3		◇ —
♣ A Q		♣ 10 9 7 6 5 4 2
	♠ J 6 2	
	♡ Q 10 8 3	
	◇ A 8 5 4	
	♣ 8 3	

North opened the ♡ A and South saw his chance to promote his trump jack (or else score his ◇ A) if he could get North to switch to a diamond. So South spectacularly played his QUEEN on North's ♡ A as a SPS, directing North to lead the higher ranking of the other two plain suits, a diamond

Superficially this queen play looks risky lest it set up an extra trick for declarer if he held ♡ J-x. But North was marked with at least five hearts by partnership agreement not to open four-card majors, so declarer held one heart at most and the queen play was safe.

North, intending to lead a trump to trick two, was startled. The ♡ Q play was a SPS asking for a diamond lead, so North instead shifted to the ◇ 10 which dummy ruffed, accepting the fatal force. West abandoned hope of bringing in dummy's great club suit and played for contract. Dummy cashed the ♡ K for the ♣ Q discard, and West ruffed a heart. Dummy ruffed a diamond, West made his ♣ A, and dummy ruffed a third diamond. West ruffed high another club and pushed high trumps to drive out the jack. West also lost a diamond trick but scored ten tricks for contract.

At most other tables West made 4 ♠ with two extra tricks. North led the ♡ A, and with no SPS to guide him, shifted to a trump. One South player did make a SPS with the ♡ 10 on ace, but North missed the signal; and he too shifted to a spade.

Dummy cashed the ♡ K for the ♣ Q discard. West made the ♣ A, dummy won a trump lead, and West ruffed high a club. The third trump lead put dummy in for the last time, but it drew South's last trump and dummy ran the good clubs to let West get plenty discards to score two extra tricks.

This deal was sent to me by Mrs. Virginia LeVey of Rochester, New York, who found the winning defense. She is a member of the American Bridge Teachers' Association.

Deal 79 Solution Preferred Practice 5 ♡ by West

♠ K Q 9 7
♡ —
◇ Q 9 6 5 2
♣ 9 6 3 2

♠ 2
♡ Q 10 8 6 5 4 3
◇ A 8
♣ K J 4

♠ 6 4 3
♡ K J 7 2
◇ J 4
♣ A Q 10 7

♠ A J 10 8 5
♡ A 9
◇ K 10 7 3
♣ 8 5

North led the ♠ K. Unlucky expert in South put on the ♠ jack as a suit-preference signal, asking for a diamond shift. But North lapsed and led another spade that declarer ruffed. Declarer lost his ♡ K to South's ♡ A. South led a diamond, but it was too late. Declarer won with the ◇ A, drew trump, and ditched his diamond loser on his fourth club trick; and made 5 ♡.

South can read North's 4 ♠ jump as showing at least four spades, placing one at most in West. So South should do his own work the 100% way of having it done right, and overtake the ♠ K with the ace and switch to a diamond at once. Signals are vital but they should be used only when the defense has no other recourse.

Compare with Deal 61, Do It Yourself; and Deal 73, Judgement.

Deal 80 Solution Call for Insurance 5 ♣ by West

West	North	East
	♠ J 8 6 ♡ A K Q 10 8 ◇ 8 6 4 3 ♣ 4	
♠ A ♡ 6 4 3 ◇ K J ♣ A Q J 9 8 7 3		♠ K Q 10 5 ♡ J 5 ◇ A Q 10 9 2 ♣ 10 5
	♠ 9 7 4 3 2 ♡ 9 7 2 ◇ 7 5 ♣ K 6 2	

When North leads the ♡ K then ♡ Q, South should play his seven then deuce, a high-low or echo asking North to lead another heart. The usual purpose of an echo is to show a doubleton with desire to ruff, perhaps to show a top card; but here South wants dummy forced in order to stop a second and fatal finesse through his trump king. Here the echo is a call for insurance on the setting trick, the trump king.

WARNING! After declarer ruffs the third heart in dummy and wins one trump finesse, he runs diamonds. South must resist all temptation to trump any diamond lest he lose his trump king.

Deal 81 Solution Into the Teeth 4 ♠ by West

	North	
	♠ 6	
	♡ 8 6 5 4 2	
	◇ J 9 3	
	♣ Q J 10 5	
♠ A K J 4 2		♠ Q 10 8 3
♡ 10 7		♡ Q J 9 3
◇ 10 7 4		◇ A Q 8 5
♠ K 7 3		♣ 2
	♠ 9 7 5	
	♡ A K	
	◇ K 6 2	
	♣ A 9 8 6 4	

North leads ♣ Q to South's ♣ A. If North had opened a diamond instead, the contract would have been a cinch to break, but South was not so lucky.

South has three defense tricks, his ♣ A already won and ♡ A-K, so he needs another trick somewhere to break the contract. Clearly the bidding shows North with no high honor and the only hope is to promote a third-round diamond trick. South should make the idiotic-looking lead of a diamond into the teeth of dummy's ◇ A-Q-8-5! If North holds ◇ J-10-x or ◇ J-9-x, South has enough time to establish and score his vital diamond trick before declarer can establish dummy's heart suit for a diamond discard.

Deal 82 Solution Dramatic Discard 4 ♠ by East

	♠ 10 3 ♡ 10 9 ♢ 8 7 5 2 ♣ A K 9 7 2	
♠ J 7 6 2 ♡ Q J 4 ♢ K 9 4 ♣ 10 6 3		♠ A K 9 8 5 ♡ A K 8 7 2 ♢ — ♣ J 8 4
	♠ Q 4 ♡ 6 5 3 ♢ A Q J 10 6 3 ♣ Q 5	

Newspaper bridge columnist Alfred P. Sheinwold reported that Harry Fishbein, playing South, opened the ♣ Q that won. Next North won the ♣ K, then ♣ A. Apparently Fishbein & Partner were not playing discard SPS's. East had bid both major suits and had followed suit on three club leads, so was probably void of diamonds. Hence Fishbein's ♢ A had a futile future trickwise.

If Fishbein discarded a low heart, he would get a diamond lead; and vice-versa. Neatly he solved his dilemma by making the dramatic discard of the ♢ A! This in face of dummy's ♢ K forced North to the right conclusion, a CLUB return that let South score his trump queen **en passant.**

Defenders using discard SPS's do not need the violent ♢ A discard to direct a club lead. South can discard the ♡ 3 to direct the lead of the lower ranking of the other two plain suits, a club. Or instead South can discard his lowest diamond, the three, to show preference for a club lead.

Deal 83 Solution Stop That Squeeze! 6 NT by East

♠ Q 10 8 6 2
♡ 8 6 5
◇ 7 4
♣ Q 10 3

West	East
♠ A 5	♠ J 7 3
♡ A Q J 3	♡ K 10 4
◇ A Q J 2	◇ K 10 6
♣ K J 9	♣ A 5 4 2

♠ K 9 4
♡ 9 7 2
◇ 9 8 5 3
♣ 8 7 6

North opens ♠ 6, dummy plays ♠ 7, and South should insert the NINE! By the Rule of Eleven South counts West for only one spade higher than the six. From honors in South's view, West's 22 high-card points to open 2 NT must include the ♠ A or ♠ Q, or 24 points include the ♠ A. The ♠ 9 insert could lose the slam if West holds the ♠ Q but percentages favor his holding the ♠ A.

The ♠ 9 wins! But to trick two South must return the ♠ 4, NOT HIS KING. South holds no value in any other suit and so he must relieve his partner of guarding spades in the end game. North must be free to discard ALL his spades to avoid a possible squeeze.

If South returns the ♠ K to West's ♠ A to trick two, West's eighth red-suit winner finds North with ♠ Q and ♣ Q-10-3 and an impossible discard to make. North, under the hammer of ♠ J and ♣ A-5-2 in dummy, will have to discard first; and declarer will make his slam.

THE END

A CATALOGUE OF SELECTED DOVER BOOKS IN ALL FIELDS OF INTEREST

A CATALOGUE OF SELECTED DOVER BOOKS IN ALL FIELDS OF INTEREST

CONDITIONED REFLEXES, Ivan P. Pavlov. Full translation of most complete statement of Pavlov's work; cerebral damage, conditioned reflex, experiments with dogs, sleep, similar topics of great importance. 430pp. 5⅜ x 8½. 60614-7 Pa. $4.50

NOTES ON NURSING: WHAT IT IS, AND WHAT IT IS NOT, Florence Nightingale. Outspoken writings by founder of modern nursing. When first published (1860) it played an important role in much needed revolution in nursing. Still stimulating. 140pp. 5⅜ x 8½. 22340-X Pa. $2.50

HARTER'S PICTURE ARCHIVE FOR COLLAGE AND ILLUSTRATION, Jim Harter. Over 300 authentic, rare 19th-century engravings selected by noted collagist for artists, designers, decoupeurs, etc. Machines, people, animals, etc., printed one side of page. 25 scene plates for backgrounds. 6 collages by Harter, Satty, Singer, Evans. Introduction. 192pp. 8⅞ x 11¾. 23659-5 Pa. $5.00

MANUAL OF TRADITIONAL WOOD CARVING, edited by Paul N. Hasluck. Possibly the best book in English on the craft of wood carving. Practical instructions, along with 1,146 working drawings and photographic illustrations. Formerly titled *Cassell's Wood Carving*. 576pp. 6½ x 9¼. 23489-4 Pa. $7.95

THE PRINCIPLES AND PRACTICE OF HAND OR SIMPLE TURNING, John Jacob Holtzapffel. Full coverage of basic lathe techniques—history and development, special apparatus, softwood turning, hardwood turning, metal turning. Many projects—billiard ball, works formed within a sphere, egg cups, ash trays, vases, jardiniers, others—included. 1881 edition. 800 illustrations. 592pp. 6⅛ x 9¼. 23365-0 Clothbd. $15.00

THE JOY OF HANDWEAVING, Osma Tod. Only book you need for hand weaving. Fundamentals, threads, weaves, plus numerous projects for small board-loom, two-harness, tapestry, laid-in, four-harness weaving and more. Over 160 illustrations. 2nd revised edition. 352pp. 6½ x 9¼. 23458-4 Pa. $5.00

THE BOOK OF WOOD CARVING, Charles Marshall Sayers. Still finest book for beginning student in wood sculpture. Noted teacher, craftsman discusses fundamentals, technique; gives 34 designs, over 34 projects for panels, bookends, mirrors, etc. "Absolutely first-rate"—E. J. Tangerman. 33 photos. 118pp. 7¾ x 10⅝. 23654-4 Pa. $3.00

DRAWINGS OF WILLIAM BLAKE, William Blake. 92 plates from Book of Job, *Divine Comedy, Paradise Lost,* visionary heads, mythological figures, Laocoon, etc. Selection, introduction, commentary by Sir Geoffrey Keynes. 178pp. 8⅛ x 11. 22303-5 Pa. $4.00

ENGRAVINGS OF HOGARTH, William Hogarth. 101 of Hogarth's greatest works: *Rake's Progress, Harlot's Progress, Illustrations for Hudibras, Before and After, Beer Street and Gin Lane,* many more. Full commentary. 256pp. 11 x 13¾. 22479-1 Pa. $7.95

DAUMIER: 120 GREAT LITHOGRAPHS, Honore Daumier. Wide-ranging collection of lithographs by the greatest caricaturist of the 19th century. Concentrates on eternally popular series on lawyers, on married life, on liberated women, etc. Selection, introduction, and notes on plates by Charles F. Ramus. Total of 158pp. 9⅜ x 12¼. 23512-2 Pa. $5.50

DRAWINGS OF MUCHA, Alphonse Maria Mucha. Work reveals draftsman of highest caliber: studies for famous posters and paintings, renderings for book illustrations and ads, etc. 70 works, 9 in color; including 6 items not drawings. Introduction. List of illustrations. 72pp. 9⅜ x 12¼. (Available in U.S. only) 23672-2 Pa. $4.00

GIOVANNI BATTISTA PIRANESI: DRAWINGS IN THE PIERPONT MORGAN LIBRARY, Giovanni Battista Piranesi. For first time ever all of Morgan Library's collection, world's largest. 167 illustrations of rare Piranesi drawings—archeological, architectural, decorative and visionary. Essay, detailed list of drawings, chronology, captions. Edited by Felice Stampfle. 144pp. 9⅜ x 12¼. 23714-1 Pa. $7.50

NEW YORK ETCHINGS (1905-1949), John Sloan. All of important American artist's N.Y. life etchings. 67 works include some of his best art; also lively historical record—Greenwich Village, tenement scenes. Edited by Sloan's widow. Introduction and captions. 79pp. 8⅜ x 11¼. 23651-X Pa. $4.00

CHINESE PAINTING AND CALLIGRAPHY: A PICTORIAL SURVEY, Wan-go Weng. 69 fine examples from John M. Crawford's matchless private collection: landscapes, birds, flowers, human figures, etc., plus calligraphy. Every basic form included: hanging scrolls, handscrolls, album leaves, fans, etc. 109 illustrations. Introduction. Captions. 192pp. 8⅞ x 11¾. 23707-9 Pa. $7.95

DRAWINGS OF REMBRANDT, edited by Seymour Slive. Updated Lippmann, Hofstede de Groot edition, with definitive scholarly apparatus. All portraits, biblical sketches, landscapes, nudes, Oriental figures, classical studies, together with selection of work by followers. 550 illustrations. Total of 630pp. 9⅛ x 12¼. 21485-0, 21486-9 Pa., Two-vol. set $15.00

THE DISASTERS OF WAR, Francisco Goya. 83 etchings record horrors of Napoleonic wars in Spain and war in general. Reprint of 1st edition, plus 3 additional plates. Introduction by Philip Hofer. 97pp. 9⅜ x 8¼. 21872-4 Pa. $3.75

THE EARLY WORK OF AUBREY BEARDSLEY, Aubrey Beardsley. 157 plates, 2 in color: *Manon Lescaut, Madame Bovary, Morte Darthur, Salome,* other. Introduction by H. Marillier. 182pp. 8⅛ x 11. 21816-3 Pa. $4.50

THE LATER WORK OF AUBREY BEARDSLEY, Aubrey Beardsley. Exotic masterpieces of full maturity: *Venus and Tannhauser, Lysistrata, Rape of the Lock, Volpone,* Savoy material, etc. 174 plates, 2 in color. 186pp. 8⅛ x 11. 21817-1 Pa. $4.50

THOMAS NAST'S CHRISTMAS DRAWINGS, Thomas Nast. Almost all Christmas drawings by creator of image of Santa Claus as we know it, and one of America's foremost illustrators and political cartoonists. 66 illustrations. 3 illustrations in color on covers. 96pp. 8⅜ x 11¼. 23660-9 Pa. $3.50

THE DORÉ ILLUSTRATIONS FOR DANTE'S DIVINE COMEDY, Gustave Doré. All 135 plates from Inferno, Purgatory, Paradise; fantastic tortures, infernal landscapes, celestial wonders. Each plate with appropriate (translated) verses. 141pp. 9 x 12. 23231-X Pa. $4.50

DORÉ'S ILLUSTRATIONS FOR RABELAIS, Gustave Doré. 252 striking illustrations of *Gargantua and Pantagruel* books by foremost 19th-century illustrator. Including 60 plates, 192 delightful smaller illustrations. 153pp. 9 x 12. 23656-0 Pa. $5.00

LONDON: A PILGRIMAGE, Gustave Doré, Blanchard Jerrold. Squalor, riches, misery, beauty of mid-Victorian metropolis; 55 wonderful plates, 125 other illustrations, full social, cultural text by Jerrold. 191pp. of text. 9⅜ x 12¼. 22306-X Pa. $6.00

THE RIME OF THE ANCIENT MARINER, Gustave Doré, S. T. Coleridge. Dore's finest work, 34 plates capture moods, subtleties of poem. Full text. Introduction by Millicent Rose. 77pp. 9¼ x 12. 22305-1 Pa. $3.50

THE DORE BIBLE ILLUSTRATIONS, Gustave Doré. All wonderful, detailed plates: Adam and Eve, Flood, Babylon, Life of Jesus, etc. Brief King James text with each plate. Introduction by Millicent Rose. 241 plates. 241pp. 9 x 12. 23004-X Pa. $6.00

THE COMPLETE ENGRAVINGS, ETCHINGS AND DRYPOINTS OF ALBRECHT DURER. "Knight, Death and Devil"; "Melencolia," and more—all Dürer's known works in all three media, including 6 works formerly attributed to him. 120 plates. 235pp. 8⅜ x 11¼. 22851-7 Pa. $6.50

MAXIMILIAN'S TRIUMPHAL ARCH, Albrecht Dürer and others. Incredible monument of woodcut art: 8 foot high elaborate arch—heraldic figures, humans, battle scenes, fantastic elements—that you can assemble yourself. Printed on one side, layout for assembly. 143pp. 11 x 16. 21451-6 Pa. $5.00

THE COMPLETE WOODCUTS OF ALBRECHT DURER, edited by Dr. W. Kurth. 346 in all: "Old Testament," "St. Jerome," "Passion," "Life of Virgin," Apocalypse," many others. Introduction by Campbell Dodgson. 285pp. 8½ x 12¼. 21097-9 Pa. $6.95

DRAWINGS OF ALBRECHT DURER, edited by Heinrich Wolfflin. 81 plates show development from youth to full style. Many favorites; many new. Introduction by Alfred Werner. 96pp. 8⅛ x 11. 22352-3 Pa. $5.00

THE HUMAN FIGURE, Albrecht Dürer. Experiments in various techniques—stereometric, progressive proportional, and others. Also life studies that rank among finest ever done. Complete reprinting of *Dresden Sketchbook*. 170 plates. 355pp. 8⅜ x 11¼. 21042-1 Pa. $7.95

OF THE JUST SHAPING OF LETTERS, Albrecht Dürer. Renaissance artist explains design of Roman majuscules by geometry, also Gothic lower and capitals. Grolier Club edition. 43pp. 7⅞ x 10¾ 21306-4 Pa. $3.00

TEN BOOKS ON ARCHITECTURE, Vitruvius. The most important book ever written on architecture. Early Roman aesthetics, technology, classical orders, site selection, all other aspects. Stands behind everything since. Morgan translation. 331pp. 5⅜ x 8½. 20645-9 Pa. $4.00

THE FOUR BOOKS OF ARCHITECTURE, Andrea Palladio. 16th-century classic responsible for Palladian movement and style. Covers classical architectural remains, Renaissance revivals, classical orders, etc. 1738 Ware English edition. Introduction by A. Placzek. 216 plates. 110pp. of text. 9½ x 12¾. 21308-0 Pa. $8.95

HORIZONS, Norman Bel Geddes. Great industrialist stage designer, "father of streamlining," on application of aesthetics to transportation, amusement, architecture, etc. 1932 prophetic account; function, theory, specific projects. 222 illustrations. 312pp. 7⅞ x 10¾. 23514-9 Pa. $6.95

FRANK LLOYD WRIGHT'S FALLINGWATER, Donald Hoffmann. Full, illustrated story of conception and building of Wright's masterwork at Bear Run, Pa. 100 photographs of site, construction, and details of completed structure. 112pp. 9¼ x 10. 23671-4 Pa. $5.00

THE ELEMENTS OF DRAWING, John Ruskin. Timeless classic by great Viltorian; starts with basic ideas, works through more difficult. Many practical exercises. 48 illustrations. Introduction by Lawrence Campbell. 228pp. 5⅜ x 8½. 22730-8 Pa. $2.75

GIST OF ART, John Sloan. Greatest modern American teacher, Art Students League, offers innumerable hints, instructions, guided comments to help you in painting. Not a formal course. 46 illustrations. Introduction by Helen Sloan. 200pp. 5⅜ x 8½. 23435-5 Pa. $3.50

THE ANATOMY OF THE HORSE, George Stubbs. Often considered the great masterpiece of animal anatomy. Full reproduction of 1766 edition, plus prospectus; original text and modernized text. 36 plates. Introduction by Eleanor Garvey. 121pp. 11 x 14¾. 23402-9 Pa. $6.00

BRIDGMAN'S LIFE DRAWING, George B. Bridgman. More than 500 illustrative drawings and text teach you to abstract the body into its major masses, use light and shade, proportion; as well as specific areas of anatomy, of which Bridgman is master. 192pp. 6½ x 9¼. (Available in U.S. only) 22710-3 Pa. $3.00

ART NOUVEAU DESIGNS IN COLOR, Alphonse Mucha, Maurice Verneuil, Georges Auriol. Full-color reproduction of *Combinaisons ornementales* (c. 1900) by Art Nouveau masters. Floral, animal, geometric, interlacings, swashes—borders, frames, spots—all incredibly beautiful. 60 plates, hundreds of designs. 9⅜ x 8-1/16. 22885-1 Pa. $4.00

FULL-COLOR FLORAL DESIGNS IN THE ART NOUVEAU STYLE, E. A. Seguy. 166 motifs, on 40 plates, from *Les fleurs et leurs applications decoratives* (1902): borders, circular designs, repeats, allovers, "spots." All in authentic Art Nouveau colors. 48pp. 9⅜ x 12¼. 23439-8 Pa. $5.00

A DIDEROT PICTORIAL ENCYCLOPEDIA OF TRADES AND INDUSTRY, edited by Charles C. Gillispie. 485 most interesting plates from the great French Encyclopedia of the 18th century show hundreds of working figures, artifacts, process, land and cityscapes; glassmaking, papermaking, metal extraction, construction, weaving, making furniture, clothing, wigs, dozens of other activities. Plates fully explained. 920pp. 9 x 12. 22284-5, 22285-3 Clothbd., Two-vol. set $40.00

HANDBOOK OF EARLY ADVERTISING ART, Clarence P. Hornung. Largest collection of copyright-free early and antique advertising art ever compiled. Over 6,000 illustrations, from Franklin's time to the 1890's for special effects, novelty. Valuable source, almost inexhaustible.
Pictorial Volume. Agriculture, the zodiac, animals, autos, birds, Christmas, fire engines, flowers, trees, musical instruments, ships, games and sports, much more. Arranged by subject matter and use. 237 plates. 288pp. 9 x 12. 20122-8 Clothbd. $13.50

Typographical Volume. Roman and Gothic faces ranging from 10 point to 300 point, "Barnum," German and Old English faces, script, logotypes, scrolls and flourishes, 1115 ornamental initials, 67 complete alphabets, more. 310 plates. 320pp. 9 x 12. 20123-6 Clothbd. $15.00

CALLIGRAPHY (CALLIGRAPHIA LATINA), J. G. Schwandner. High point of 18th-century ornamental calligraphy. Very ornate initials, scrolls, borders, cherubs, birds, lettered examples. 172pp. 9 x 13. 20475-8 Pa. $6.00

ART FORMS IN NATURE, Ernst Haeckel. Multitude of strangely beautiful natural forms: Radiolaria, Foraminifera, jellyfishes, fungi, turtles, bats, etc. All 100 plates of the 19th-century evolutionist's *Kunstformen der Natur* (1904). 100pp. 9⅜ x 12¼. 22987-4 Pa. $4.50

CHILDREN: A PICTORIAL ARCHIVE FROM NINETEENTH-CENTURY SOURCES, edited by Carol Belanger Grafton. 242 rare, copyright-free wood engravings for artists and designers. Widest such selection available. All illustrations in line. 119pp. 8⅜ x 11¼. 23694-3 Pa. $3.50

WOMEN: A PICTORIAL ARCHIVE FROM NINETEENTH-CENTURY SOURCES, edited by Jim Harter. 391 copyright-free wood engravings for artists and designers selected from rare periodicals. Most extensive such collection available. All illustrations in line. 128pp. 9 x 12. 23703-6 Pa. $4.50

ARABIC ART IN COLOR, Prisse d'Avennes. From the greatest ornamentalists of all time—50 plates in color, rarely seen outside the Near East, rich in suggestion and stimulus. Includes 4 plates on covers. 46pp. 9⅜ x 12¼. 23658-7 Pa. $6.00

AUTHENTIC ALGERIAN CARPET DESIGNS AND MOTIFS, edited by June Beveridge. Algerian carpets are world famous. Dozens of geometrical motifs are charted on grids, color-coded, for weavers, needleworkers, craftsmen, designers. 53 illustrations plus 4 in color. 48pp. 8¼ x 11. (Available in U.S. only) 23650-1 Pa. $1.75

DICTIONARY OF AMERICAN PORTRAITS, edited by Hayward and Blanche Cirker. 4000 important Americans, earliest times to 1905, mostly in clear line. Politicians, writers, soldiers, scientists, inventors, industrialists, Indians, Blacks, women, outlaws, etc. Identificatory information. 756pp. 9¼ x 12¾. 21823-6 Clothbd. $40.00

HOW THE OTHER HALF LIVES, Jacob A. Riis. Journalistic record of filth, degradation, upward drive in New York immigrant slums, shops, around 1900. New edition includes 100 original Riis photos, monuments of early photography. 233pp. 10 x 7⅞. 22012-5 Pa. $6.00

NEW YORK IN THE THIRTIES, Berenice Abbott. Noted photographer's fascinating study of city shows new buildings that have become famous and old sights that have disappeared forever. Insightful commentary. 97 photographs. 97pp. 11⅜ x 10. 22967-X Pa. $5.00

MEN AT WORK, Lewis W. Hine. Famous photographic studies of construction workers, railroad men, factory workers and coal miners. New supplement of 18 photos on Empire State building construction. New introduction by Jonathan L. Doherty. Total of 69 photos. 63pp. 8 x 10¾. 23475-4 Pa. $3.00

THE DEPRESSION YEARS AS PHOTOGRAPHED BY ARTHUR ROTHSTEIN, Arthur Rothstein. First collection devoted entirely to the work of outstanding 1930s photographer: famous dust storm photo, ragged children, unemployed, etc. 120 photographs. Captions. 119pp. 9¼ x 10¾.
23590-4 Pa. $5.00

CAMERA WORK: A PICTORIAL GUIDE, Alfred Stieglitz. All 559 illustrations and plates from the most important periodical in the history of art photography, *Camera Work* (1903-17). Presented four to a page, reduced in size but still clear, in strict chronological order, with complete captions. Three indexes. Glossary. Bibliography. 176pp. 8⅜ x 11¼.
23591-2 Pa. $6.95

ALVIN LANGDON COBURN, PHOTOGRAPHER, Alvin L. Coburn. Revealing autobiography by one of greatest photographers of 20th century gives insider's version of Photo-Secession, plus comments on his own work. 77 photographs by Coburn. Edited by Helmut and Alison Gernsheim. 160pp. 8⅛ x 11. 23685-4 Pa. $6.00

NEW YORK IN THE FORTIES, Andreas Feininger. 162 brilliant photographs by the well-known photographer, formerly with *Life* magazine, show commuters, shoppers, Times Square at night, Harlem nightclub, Lower East Side, etc. Introduction and full captions by John von Hartz. 181pp. 9¼ x 10¾. 23585-8 Pa. $6.00

GREAT NEWS PHOTOS AND THE STORIES BEHIND THEM, John Faber. Dramatic volume of 140 great news photos, 1855 through 1976, and revealing stories behind them, with both historical and technical information. Hindenburg disaster, shooting of Oswald, nomination of Jimmy Carter, etc. 160pp. 8¼ x 11. 23667-6 Pa. $5.00

THE ART OF THE CINEMATOGRAPHER, Leonard Maltin. Survey of American cinematography history and anecdotal interviews with 5 masters—Arthur Miller, Hal Mohr, Hal Rosson, Lucien Ballard, and Conrad Hall. Very large selection of behind-the-scenes production photos. 105 photographs. Filmographies. Index. Originally *Behind the Camera.* 144pp. 8¼ x 11. 23686-2 Pa. $5.00

DESIGNS FOR THE THREE-CORNERED HAT (LE TRICORNE), Pablo Picasso. 32 fabulously rare drawings—including 31 color illustrations of costumes and accessories—for 1919 production of famous ballet. Edited by Parmenia Migel, who has written new introduction. 48pp. 9⅜ x 12¼. (Available in U.S. only) 23709-5 Pa. $5.00

NOTES OF A FILM DIRECTOR, Sergei Eisenstein. Greatest Russian filmmaker explains montage, making of *Alexander Nevsky,* aesthetics; comments on self, associates, great rivals (Chaplin), similar material. 78 illustrations. 240pp. 5⅜ x 8½. 22392-2 Pa. $4.50

HOLLYWOOD GLAMOUR PORTRAITS, edited by John Kobal. 145 photos capture the stars from 1926-49, the high point in portrait photography. Gable, Harlow, Bogart, Bacall, Hedy Lamarr, Marlene Dietrich, Robert Montgomery, Marlon Brando, Veronica Lake; 94 stars in all. Full background on photographers, technical aspects, much more. Total of 160pp. 8⅜ x 11¼. 23352-9 Pa. $5.00

THE NEW YORK STAGE: FAMOUS PRODUCTIONS IN PHOTOGRAPHS, edited by Stanley Appelbaum. 148 photographs from Museum of City of New York show 142 plays, 1883-1939. *Peter Pan, The Front Page, Dead End, Our Town,* O'Neill, hundreds of actors and actresses, etc. Full indexes. 154pp. 9½ x 10. 23241-7 Pa. $6.00

MASTERS OF THE DRAMA, John Gassner. Most comprehensive history of the drama, every tradition from Greeks to modern Europe and America, including Orient. Covers 800 dramatists, 2000 plays; biography, plot summaries, criticism, theatre history, etc. 77 illustrations. 890pp. 5⅜ x 8½. 20100-7 Clothbd. $10.00

THE GREAT OPERA STARS IN HISTORIC PHOTOGRAPHS, edited by James Camner. 343 portraits from the 1850s to the 1940s: Tamburini, Mario, Caliapin, Jeritza, Melchior, Melba, Patti, Pinza, Schipa, Caruso, Farrar, Steber, Gobbi, and many more—270 performers in all. Index. 199pp. 8⅜ x 11¼. 23575-0 Pa. $6.50

J. S. BACH, Albert Schweitzer. Great full-length study of Bach, life, background to music, music, by foremost modern scholar. Ernest Newman translation. 650 musical examples. Total of 928pp. 5⅜ x 8½. (Available in U.S. only) 21631-4, 21632-2 Pa., Two-vol. set $10.00

COMPLETE PIANO SONATAS, Ludwig van Beethoven. All sonatas in the fine Schenker edition, with fingering, analytical material. One of best modern editions. Total of 615pp. 9 x 12. (Available in U.S. only) 23134-8, 23135-6 Pa., Two-vol. set $15.00

KEYBOARD MUSIC, J. S. Bach. Bach-Gesellschaft edition. For harpsichord, piano, other keyboard instruments. English Suites, French Suites, Six Partitas, Goldberg Variations, Two-Part Inventions, Three-Part Sinfonias. 312pp. 8⅛ x 11. (Available in U.S. only) 22360-4 Pa. $6.00

FOUR SYMPHONIES IN FULL SCORE, Franz Schubert. Schubert's four most popular symphonies: No. 4 in C Minor ("Tragic"); No. 5 in B-flat Major; No. 8 in B Minor ("Unfinished"); No. 9 in C Major ("Great"). Breitkopf & Hartel edition. Study score. 261pp. 9⅜ x 12¼. 23681-1 Pa. $6.50

THE AUTHENTIC GILBERT & SULLIVAN SONGBOOK, W. S. Gilbert, A. S. Sullivan. Largest selection available; 92 songs, uncut, original keys, in piano rendering approved by Sullivan. Favorites and lesser-known fine numbers. Edited with plot synopses by James Spero. 3 illustrations. 399pp. 9 x 12. 23482-7 Pa. $7.95

PRINCIPLES OF ORCHESTRATION, Nikolay Rimsky-Korsakov. Great classical orchestrator provides fundamentals of tonal resonance, progression of parts, voice and orchestra, tutti effects, much else in major document. 330pp. of musical excerpts. 489pp. 6½ x 9¼. 21266-1 Pa. $6.00

TRISTAN UND ISOLDE, Richard Wagner. Full orchestral score with complete instrumentation. Do not confuse with piano reduction. Commentary by Felix Mottl, great Wagnerian conductor and scholar. Study score. 655pp. 8⅛ x 11. 22915-7 Pa. $12.50

REQUIEM IN FULL SCORE, Giuseppe Verdi. Immensely popular with choral groups and music lovers. Republication of edition published by C. F. Peters, Leipzig, n. d. German frontmaker in English translation. Glossary. Text in Latin. Study score. 204pp. 9⅜ x 12¼.
23682-X Pa. $6.00

COMPLETE CHAMBER MUSIC FOR STRINGS, Felix Mendelssohn. All of Mendelssohn's chamber music: Octet, 2 Quintets, 6 Quartets, and Four Pieces for String Quartet. (Nothing with piano is included). Complete works edition (1874-7). Study score. 283 pp. 9⅜ x 12¼.
23679-X Pa. $6.95

POPULAR SONGS OF NINETEENTH-CENTURY AMERICA, edited by Richard Jackson. 64 most important songs: "Old Oaken Bucket," "Arkansas Traveler," "Yellow Rose of Texas," etc. Authentic original sheet music, full introduction and commentaries. 290pp. 9 x 12. 23270-0 Pa. $6.00

COLLECTED PIANO WORKS, Scott Joplin. Edited by Vera Brodsky Lawrence. Practically all of Joplin's piano works—rags, two-steps, marches, waltzes, etc., 51 works in all. Extensive introduction by Rudi Blesh. Total of 345pp. 9 x 12. 23106-2 Pa. $14.95

BASIC PRINCIPLES OF CLASSICAL BALLET, Agrippina Vaganova. Great Russian theoretician, teacher explains methods for teaching classical ballet; incorporates best from French, Italian, Russian schools. 118 illustrations. 175pp. 5⅜ x 8½. 22036-2 Pa. $2.50

CHINESE CHARACTERS, L. Wieger. Rich analysis of 2300 characters according to traditional systems into primitives. Historical-semantic analysis to phonetics (Classical Mandarin) and radicals. 820pp. 6⅛ x 9¼.
21321-8 Pa. $10.00

EGYPTIAN LANGUAGE: EASY LESSONS IN EGYPTIAN HIEROGLYPHICS, E. A. Wallis Budge. Foremost Egyptologist offers Egyptian grammar, explanation of hieroglyphics, many reading texts, dictionary of symbols. 246pp. 5 x 7½. (Available in U.S. only)
21394-3 Clothbd. $7.50

AN ETYMOLOGICAL DICTIONARY OF MODERN ENGLISH, Ernest Weekley. Richest, fullest work, by foremost British lexicographer. Detailed word histories. Inexhaustible. Do not confuse this with *Concise Etymological Dictionary,* which is abridged. Total of 856pp. 6½ x 9¼.
21873-2, 21874-0 Pa., Two-vol. set $12.00

A MAYA GRAMMAR, Alfred M. Tozzer. Practical, useful English-language grammar by the Harvard anthropologist who was one of the three greatest American scholars in the area of Maya culture. Phonetics, grammatical processes, syntax, more. 301pp. 5⅜ x 8½. 23465-7 Pa. $4.00

THE JOURNAL OF HENRY D. THOREAU, edited by Bradford Torrey, F. H. Allen. Complete reprinting of 14 volumes, 1837-61, over two million words; the sourcebooks for *Walden,* etc. Definitive. All original sketches, plus 75 photographs. Introduction by Walter Harding. Total of 1804pp. 8½ x 12¼. 20312-3, 20313-1 Clothbd., Two-vol. set $50.00

CLASSIC GHOST STORIES, Charles Dickens and others. 18 wonderful stories you've wanted to reread: "The Monkey's Paw," "The House and the Brain," "The Upper Berth," "The Signalman," "Dracula's Guest," "The Tapestried Chamber," etc. Dickens, Scott, Mary Shelley, Stoker, etc. 330pp. 5⅜ x 8½. 20735-8 Pa. $3.50

SEVEN SCIENCE FICTION NOVELS, H. G. Wells. Full novels. *First Men in the Moon, Island of Dr. Moreau, War of the Worlds, Food of the Gods, Invisible Man, Time Machine, In the Days of the Comet.* A basic science-fiction library. 1015pp. 5⅜ x 8½. (Available in U.S. only)
20264-X Clothbd. $8.95

ARMADALE, Wilkie Collins. Third great mystery novel by the author of *The Woman in White* and *The Moonstone.* Ingeniously plotted narrative shows an exceptional command of character, incident and mood. Original magazine version with 40 illustrations. 597pp. 5⅜ x 8½.
23429-0 Pa. $5.00

MASTERS OF MYSTERY, H. Douglas Thomson. The first book in English (1931) devoted to history and aesthetics of detective story. Poe, Doyle, LeFanu, Dickens, many others, up to 1930. New introduction and notes by E. F. Bleiler. 288pp. 5⅜ x 8½. (Available in U.S. only)
23606-4 Pa. $4.00

FLATLAND, E. A. Abbott. Science-fiction classic explores life of 2-D being in 3-D world. Read also as introduction to thought about hyperspace. Introduction by Banesh Hoffmann. 16 illustrations. 103pp. 5⅜ x 8½.
20001-9 Pa. $1.75

THREE SUPERNATURAL NOVELS OF THE VICTORIAN PERIOD, edited, with an introduction, by E. F. Bleiler. Reprinted complete and unabridged, three great classics of the supernatural: *The Haunted Hotel* by Wilkie Collins, *The Haunted House at Latchford* by Mrs. J. H. Riddell, and *The Lost Stradivarious* by J. Meade Falkner. 325pp. 5⅜ x 8½.
22571-2 Pa. $4.00

AYESHA: THE RETURN OF "SHE," H. Rider Haggard. Virtuoso sequel featuring the great mythic creation, Ayesha, in an adventure that is fully as good as the first book, *She.* Original magazine version, with 47 original illustrations by Maurice Greiffenhagen. 189pp. 6½ x 9¼.
23649-8 Pa. $3.50

HOUSEHOLD STORIES BY THE BROTHERS GRIMM. All the great Grimm stories: "Rumpelstiltskin," "Snow White," "Hansel and Gretel," etc., with 114 illustrations by Walter Crane. 269pp. 5⅜ x 8½.
21080-4 Pa. $3.00

SLEEPING BEAUTY, illustrated by Arthur Rackham. Perhaps the fullest, most delightful version ever, told by C. S. Evans. Rackham's best work. 49 illustrations. 110pp. 7⅞ x 10¾. 22756-1 Pa. $2.50

AMERICAN FAIRY TALES, L. Frank Baum. Young cowboy lassoes Father Time; dummy in Mr. Floman's department store window comes to life; and 10 other fairy tales. 41 illustrations by N. P. Hall, Harry Kennedy, Ike Morgan, and Ralph Gardner. 209pp. 5⅜ x 8½. 23643-9 Pa. $3.00

THE WONDERFUL WIZARD OF OZ, L. Frank Baum. Facsimile in full color of America's finest children's classic. Introduction by Martin Gardner. 143 illustrations by W. W. Denslow. 267pp. 5⅜ x 8½.
20691-2 Pa. $3.50

THE TALE OF PETER RABBIT, Beatrix Potter. The inimitable Peter's terrifying adventure in Mr. McGregor's garden, with all 27 wonderful, full-color Potter illustrations. 55pp. 4¼ x 5½. (Available in U.S. only)
22827-4 Pa. $1.25

THE STORY OF KING ARTHUR AND HIS KNIGHTS, Howard Pyle. Finest children's version of life of King Arthur. 48 illustrations by Pyle. 131pp. 6⅛ x 9¼. 21445-1 Pa. $4.95

CARUSO'S CARICATURES, Enrico Caruso. Great tenor's remarkable caricatures of self, fellow musicians, composers, others. Toscanini, Puccini, Farrar, etc. Impish, cutting, insightful. 473 illustrations. Preface by M. Sisca. 217pp. 8⅜ x 11¼. 23528-9 Pa. $6.95

PERSONAL NARRATIVE OF A PILGRIMAGE TO ALMADINAH AND MECCAH, Richard Burton. Great travel classic by remarkably colorful personality. Burton, disguised as a Moroccan, visited sacred shrines of Islam, narrowly escaping death. Wonderful observations of Islamic life, customs, personalities. 47 illustrations. Total of 959pp. 5⅜ x 8½.
21217-3, 21218-1 Pa., Two-vol. set $12.00

INCIDENTS OF TRAVEL IN YUCATAN, John L. Stephens. Classic (1843) exploration of jungles of Yucatan, looking for evidences of Maya civilization. Travel adventures, Mexican and Indian culture, etc. Total of 669pp. 5⅜ x 8½. 20926-1, 20927-X Pa., Two-vol. set $7.90

AMERICAN LITERARY AUTOGRAPHS FROM WASHINGTON IRVING TO HENRY JAMES, Herbert Cahoon, et al. Letters, poems, manuscripts of Hawthorne, Thoreau, Twain, Alcott, Whitman, 67 other prominent American authors. Reproductions, full transcripts and commentary. Plus checklist of all American Literary Autographs in The Pierpont Morgan Library. Printed on exceptionally high-quality paper. 136 illustrations. 212pp. 9⅛ x 12¼. 23548-3 Pa. $7.95

YUCATAN BEFORE AND AFTER THE CONQUEST, Diego de Landa. First English translation of basic book in Maya studies, the only significant account of Yucatan written in the early post-Conquest era. Translated by distinguished Maya scholar William Gates. Appendices, introduction, 4 maps and over 120 illustrations added by translator. 162pp. 5⅜ x 8½.
23622-6 Pa. $3.00

THE MALAY ARCHIPELAGO, Alfred R. Wallace. Spirited travel account by one of founders of modern biology. Touches on zoology, botany, ethnography, geography, and geology. 62 illustrations, maps. 515pp. 5⅜ x 8½.
20187-2 Pa. $6.95

THE DISCOVERY OF THE TOMB OF TUTANKHAMEN, Howard Carter, A. C. Mace. Accompany Carter in the thrill of discovery, as ruined passage suddenly reveals unique, untouched, fabulously rich tomb. Fascinating account, with 106 illustrations. New introduction by J. M. White. Total of 382pp. 5⅜ x 8½. (Available in U.S. only) 23500-9 Pa. $4.00

THE WORLD'S GREATEST SPEECHES, edited by Lewis Copeland and Lawrence W. Lamm. Vast collection of 278 speeches from Greeks up to present. Powerful and effective models; unique look at history. Revised to 1970. Indices. 842pp. 5⅜ x 8½. 20468-5 Pa. $8.95

THE 100 GREATEST ADVERTISEMENTS, Julian Watkins. The priceless ingredient; His master's voice; 99 44/100% pure; over 100 others. How they were written, their impact, etc. Remarkable record. 130 illustrations. 233pp. 7⅞ x 10 3/5. 20540-1 Pa. $5.00

CRUICKSHANK PRINTS FOR HAND COLORING, George Cruickshank. 18 illustrations, one side of a page, on fine-quality paper suitable for watercolors. Caricatures of people in society (c. 1820) full of trenchant wit. Very large format. 32pp. 11 x 16. 23684-6 Pa. $5.00

THIRTY-TWO COLOR POSTCARDS OF TWENTIETH-CENTURY AMERICAN ART, Whitney Museum of American Art. Reproduced in full color in postcard form are 31 art works and one shot of the museum. Calder, Hopper, Rauschenberg, others. Detachable. 16pp. 8¼ x 11.
23629-3 Pa. $2.50

MUSIC OF THE SPHERES: THE MATERIAL UNIVERSE FROM ATOM TO QUASAR SIMPLY EXPLAINED, Guy Murchie. Planets, stars, geology, atoms, radiation, relativity, quantum theory, light, antimatter, similar topics. 319 figures. 664pp. 5⅜ x 8½.
21809-0, 21810-4 Pa., Two-vol. set $10.00

EINSTEIN'S THEORY OF RELATIVITY, Max Born. Finest semi-technical account; covers Einstein, Lorentz, Minkowski, and others, with much detail, much explanation of ideas and math not readily available elsewhere on this level. For student, non-specialist. 376pp. 5⅜ x 8½.
60769-0 Pa. $4.50